LOVE

Party of One

*Surviving the Pitfalls of Dating and
Relationships in a Loveless World*

KEVIN HUNTER

WARRIOR
OF LIGHT
PRESS
Los Angeles, California

Warrior of Light Press
www.kevin-hunter.com

Self-Help/Relationships
Self-Help/Dating
Spirituality/Inspiration & Personal Growth

DEDICATION

This is for those struggling in love while continuing to keep the faith in believing in the probability of it. I understand what it's like to long and dream of a healthy loving relationship that lasts a lifetime and how that can feel challenging to obtain. It is possible as I've been that tennis ball bouncing from one side of the court as a struggling single, to the other side of that court by having that encompassing love relationship one dreams of.

Thank you to all the subjects who shared their love and relationship struggles and made contributions towards my research for this book.

CHAPTERS

INTRODUCTION

Love Credentials

*T*he majority of my published works to date are spiritually based empowerment books called the *Warrior of Light* series of books. They are infused with practical messages and guidance that my Spirit team has taught and shared with me revolving around many different topics. The main goal of those books is to fine tune your body, mind, and soul. This improves humanity one person at a time. You are a Divine communicator and perfectly adjusted and capable of receiving messages from spirit as anyone else in the world.

One of the top two questions I receive from readers surrounds the topics of love and relationships, while the other revolves around career. Love and relationships are a major concern and theme for so many people. The struggles one wades through in attempting to navigate through a loveless world has made love challenging to obtain or keep.

Although the bulk of material I've written are spiritually based empowerment works, I have nevertheless been out in the relationship and dating field my entire life. Not only was I born having a basic understanding of the human condition, but I also came here as a love guide. I've taken this knowledge out into the dating field studying, researching, and interviewing countless people about their ordeals in the love department. I love all things love. I, along with my Spirit team, enjoy seeing people investing in happy committed love bonds because this world doesn't have enough love in it as it is. I've also been out in the field dating and having relationships of various levels from short term, to long term, to committed, to non-committed. I've had sexual encounters and one night stands. I've had the kind of love that others dream about, but never obtain. I've experienced what it's like to be a natural Don Juan Casanova type. I've sat down, discussed, and counseled people from all walks of life about their tribulations of being single, dating, and in love relationships.

My entire life has been devoted to all circumstances revolving around the word love. Others have commented how comfortable they feel around me enough to reveal their deepest and darkest issues that include all things connected to love relationships. When others are with me they have protested they are divulging information they wouldn't normally say to anyone else. Through this process, I've gained extensive knowledge of the difficulties that many are faced with in the current modern day dating world. I understand the practical realities that exist, but I also have spiritual knowledge, guidance, and wisdom to share as to how that applies to the souls of today on Earth.

Heartbreak is an equal opportunity killer regardless if you're male, female, gay, straight, bi, or whatever you identify to be in this lifetime. In the end, it is irrelevant since all human souls experience the same heartbreak and rejection issues as any other. There hasn't been one person who has never been slighted by love. If there is I would love to meet that person.

One of my first published pieces was a story loosely based on true accounts on having a crush on someone in my book, *Jagger's Revolution*. It was partially autobiographical and partially thrown in drama at the beginning of my career as an author. This is where the lines are blurred to the extent that it would be difficult to detect which is real and what is fiction. I've also written a spiritually based book on love and relationships that is the opposite end of that spectrum called, *Soul Mates and Twin Flames.*

I've been studying, researching, experimenting, and counseling people on love and relationships since my teenage years. I've also assisted countless numbers of people through the treacherous waters of romance. This is regardless of my own personal love life trajectory. I have definitely walked into challenging personal love relationship situations knowing what I'm getting myself into.

As a lifelong incurable romantic and love addict, I love all things connected to LOVE. It far supersedes the opposite extreme, which is lonely, isolating, addicting, and disconnected. I've always admired couples that have been together for decades and yet continue to remain loving and supportive with one another.

I wanted to write a book that centered around the realities of dating in today's challenging technologically based world and what it's like without sugar coating it. I'm not one who glosses over the darkness no matter what the content is. What sometimes comes out of me as a strong opinion is divinely guided from my Wise One spiritual team, but put into my own words. The information I convey with almost an assault like quality at times is from above to help others navigate through the distressing waters they might find themselves in.

Love Party of One is not necessarily a spiritually based book, even though there may be some hints of it sprinkled throughout, but much of the practical input is divinely guided through a sense of clear knowing, otherwise known as Claircognizance and clear hearing through my Clairaudience channel. The content includes the practical hardships others have faced in the love and relationship world and what to expect if you're embarking into your teenage years, young adulthood, or new to the current dating relationship world. There are many people who have faced the ending of a long term relationship. These are connections that have lasted years and some even decades. They head back out there into the dating world only to discover it's vastly changed. This may shed some light on the way things have become.

~ Kevin Hunter

CHAPTER ONE

SURVIVING SINGLEHOOD

Remember when people used to hold hands instead of their phones? I can do both since I'm a whiz when it comes to multi-tasking. When your business was in trouble, you found ways to save it or improve it before walking away, but you don't observe that same rule when it comes to your relationships do you? You don't put in that same fight and investment into building something solid. There are a small minority of people who do and you might be one of them. Someone who isn't interested in love and relationships will unlikely read anything surrounding the topic.

Some souls are born this lifetime with a greater detachment to emotion, but even they long for some form of companionship even if it comes in the guise of a pet or through friendships.

When you exit this Earthly plane, you leave your job behind, but the lessons and connections you made with others are what you recall that live on. Whether you are a believer of a higher power, an afterlife or not, why would you waste time not finding a space where love exists? There is nothing joyful about hanging out in an area that has zero love, yet the space that others fall prone to is one of negativity.

Life can be a struggle as you forge on, head down, eyes forward, moving with determination to survive. Your soul desires the kind of rejoicing release that love offers. When you're operating from a high vibration state, then you can come pretty close to that all encompassing all giving love that is fired off from the source naturally. Human souls rely on one another to prop each other up and give a little of bit of that love essence that exists when you reach that high state, but that puts too much pressure on connections that cannot withstand the kind of love that is required as fuel to carry on. You have to stretch higher than that in order to touch the tail end of it. The Earth's dense atmosphere compresses this love due to the domination of the darkness of the ego. It's only when you've re-entered the gates of home does your soul explode by the infusion of this love that permanently baptizes you in its light.

All human souls have an ego with varying shades of light and dark. It's the darkness of ego that causes the most unnecessary chaos. It prompts others to antagonize, attack, criticize, judge, hate, and all the cousins of those words. The world in general is loveless. This is primarily witnessed and absorbed on a massive scale all over the media. Comments posted are filled with bickering, attacking, confronting, and disagreeing with hostility and negativity. It's all noise that does nothing to positively serve, assist, or change anything. None of that is helpful and nor does it convince someone who disagrees with one's argument. All it does is breed negativity which is absorbed by others and then passed around to one another like poison seeping into your blood.

If this is what the current general population of humanity is like, then it's no wonder there are many struggling to find love in any form. Being in that space does not attract in love. There is no room for someone else's opinion or choices that differ from your own to begin with. Having a warm inviting openness is what attracts in positive circumstances to you including love. You start with you and then work your way out. You change the way you view circumstances and project that outwardly. You accept others for their differences, values, and choices even if you personally or morally disagree.

When two people merge into the right healthy committed loving union, both of the lights in their souls expand and their vibrations rise. There is no limit to what you are able to accomplish individually while in that soul connection. Love is the main reason all are here. People gravitate towards this concept because deep down most everyone longs to have that kind of a connection if they don't already have it. Most everyone has made that one bond with somebody that pulls you out of yourself completely. Some have that one great love that is never experienced again, while others move through life and never connect with another human soul in an intensely deep way. This is about reciprocated relationships and not unrequited ones.

Unrequited connections are where you have a crush or romantic interest in someone who does not share the same feelings and attraction for you. It can be someone you are in a relationship with who either was never fully into you and settled, or their feelings shifted over the course of the relationship where they no longer have romantic feelings for you. Love relationships experience peaks and valleys, so this is not uncommon. When you're with someone around the clock, then eventually it may feel as if you're both stuck in a rut or you've become a comfortable pair of old shoes. This is why relationships take work and effort to continue to keep it interesting, passionate, and thriving.

A requited deep soul connection is where you understand one another more than any other experience you've had with anybody else. It is the kind of union that you never forget and nor does it ever go away no matter how much you attempt to disregard it. This is the kind of rare connection that leaves you haunted by it decades later long after it ends. Your mind always drifts back to that profound tie you had with them. It is one that is never repeated with anyone else. The relationship might not have lasted due to various factors, but often times it's something trivial where one or the both of you allowed your ego to rule your life. When you use little ego, then circumstances function with minimal issues. The ego is selfish and makes decisions based on self-centeredness that can result in crumbling a union.

Selfishness is one of the top causes of relationship sabotage. Selfishness comes from the dark part of your ego. There are varying shades of the ego that range from the light to the dark. The light side of your ego is believing in yourself, loving all that you are, and having confidence. Relationships require selflessness, which is a quality lacking in today's modern day world in general, let alone in a love relationship. The ego wants what it desires, even if it triggers damage to a deep soul connection. Soul connections are no accident, but are predestined and determined to make

4

contact with one another this lifetime. A soul mate is a soul connection that pushes your buttons and helps you positively change and grow. Soul mate soul connections assist in one's personal and spiritual growth.

It takes me a long time to come around, but all of my romantic connections have always been forceful and intensely close. This is what happens when you merge in with a love addict. I use the term 'love addict' loosely and in an exaggerated way to imply that I love being in love and being in positive love relationships. The true meaning of the love addict is someone who is in love with the intoxicating high of the initial getting to know someone part, but then once it grows familiar they discard them and move onto the next victim. I don't do that, but rather grow stronger and more connected with the one I'm with.

The reason it has taken me time in the past to come around is because I've never jumped into a relationship with anyone on a whim. I've always taken my love relationships seriously including the coming together part. I need to be sure about them before I commit, because when I do it's for life. However, in the past, I had found those that rushed the commitment were just as rushed to end it. They did this with all those they were with, therefore do not take love relationships seriously. It is impossible to be with me and not believe it's going to be deep or intense, because it will be. It's just the way it is. The love continues to grow more concentrated as time goes by. If a connection moves into superficiality or distrust, then it will break apart. Have zero tolerance for superficiality in love. Have the mantra of putting in all or nothing. This means you put in 110% into whatever you choose to commit to or don't bother. Don't waste energy on something that you only have half an interest in because it will show.

I can see what is going on underneath and what is unsaid with someone. This has its positives and negatives. The positives are that it tells me what the other person needs. The negatives are when you see something that can make you question who you're with. One of the worst places to be is in a loveless relationship. This squeezes out all traces of oxygen and ultimately brings about suffocation. It is one of the worst love crimes you can commit next to cheating and abuse of any kind.

It's the human condition to feel bouts of loneliness or crave a passionate sexual emerging with a love partner. The reality is that being single for a prolonged period of time sucks for some people, while others have an easier time making the best of it and will live their daily life without that craving for a love relationship. The rest struggle to survive being alone.

If you can't change your relationship status tomorrow, then get with the program of the current dating market and protect yourself with the way it is now. Have a greater understanding of how the modern day world of dating and relationships are at this point in Earth's history. Do your best to make the most of the state you're currently in. This is about making sounder decisions and learning to treat others with respect. This carries far into one's life where you can apply common sense etiquette to most anything.

You might be someone who loves being single and has no problem with it, or you might be someone who desires a love partner. The longer it takes to obtain one, the more it feels as if you're trying to survive being single when you anxiously want to be in a relationship. You desperately wish you had a lover who loved you back with equal fervor, yet any and all potential prospects constantly evade you.

One of the ways of surviving modern day dating and relationships in a loveless world is by armoring yourself with knowledge. This includes knowledge over the way things currently are. You can read all of the love and relationship self-help books available on the market and still feel nowhere closer to obtaining a love relationship than you are now. You've went to psychic readers, you've cast spells, you put yourself out there, did the vision boards, the crystal meditations, and other love rituals presented to you, but you still find you're desperately wishing the person of your dreams was here already. You begin to grow more cynical as you grow older feeling as if it will never happen and that you just have to accept the fact that perhaps it's not in the cards.

You've grown permanently negative about not being able to attract in a love partner, so you debunk the tips that all of the love related self-help books have offered you. You're angry, frustrated, and over it. It's understandable that you've grown weary from battle in the love department, but this is not going to attract a stranger to you who could be the potential mate. You'll also stop bothering to put in an effort as you've grown exhausted over the process. I don't blame you as I've been there too and get it. I've had periods throughout my life where I've had to survive being single. When each of my past long term love relationships ended, I would believe that was it. There would be no one else after that. As time progressed on, and I seemed to be in a place of contentment, then a new soul mate would enter the picture. Rinse and repeat. It was anything but over for me.

Perhaps none of the tips you've been given work for you, but isn't it better to apply positive attributes, tips, and traits to one's life rather than living in misery? I don't know about you, but I have zero tolerance for sitting in the same room with a negative complainer or gossip. I warm up immediately to someone who is warm, friendly, sociable, and inviting…no matter how physically attractive or unattractive they might be. This is to further hammer home that in the end physical beauty is not always a primary factor for everybody. While it certainly helps as some say that you be physically attracted to the person, but it doesn't keep someone interested. It doesn't have staying power if there are no other similarities, interests, communication styles, and values.

Display positive qualities right off the bat. Friendly eye contact with a smile and a warm hello can go a long way. You also feel good and uplifted when it's returned in kind. This energy raises your vibration, which assists in attracting positive circumstances to you. A high vibration equates to a stronger connection with an energy force greater than yourself. The positive energy prompts others to pick up on it and turn their head to notice you.

CHAPTER TWO

LOVELESS DATING WORLD

*L*ove is where all human souls are intended and expected to be, but most have strayed as far away from that space as possible. They've fallen victim to the mundane practical stresses of life, struggling to make a living, pay bills, buying groceries, and whatever it takes to survive in day-to-day functioning. Secretly somewhere deep down in that person's soul they long for some measure of a personal life that brings in a welcome relief and release in the form of a love partner. By the time you're done working you're too exhausted to sit face to face with another stranger, so you take the slim pickings that come to you seriously. You won't go out with just anyone who hits you up simply because they're attractive.

During my research, I've found that the many potentials that hit me up seemed to have too much time on their hands. They limit their messages to you in a series of one to three-word sound bite phrases while expecting to meet in ten minutes. This shotgun method of connecting with others doesn't work and nor does it bring you quality connections. For one, these are prospects that don't have anything going for them, which is why they have an abnormal amount of free time on their hands. Usually when someone wants to meet that quickly is because they only have one thing in mind, and that is to ultimately get it on. This is one of the downfalls to the app method of connecting. There is no way to filter out prospects by professionals or those with likeminded interests. You basically get everyone and their family hitting you up.

When someone is longing to connect with a long term relationship potential, one of the qualities they look for in another is someone who seems to have their life together with goals, aspirations, and dreams their diving into or working towards. They're not sitting around the house each day bored witless. They understand the value of gradually building a connection with someone of quality. They are looking for potentials that have some positive measure of an existence that includes life path and purpose goals they are working towards. If a random stranger hits you up with, "I'm bored", then what do you think you're going to get? How many successful executives in the world would utter that phrase or be attracted to someone like that? At the same time, you don't want to be incredibly busy for months that you have no time to meet with someone new or develop a bond with them.

In the early 1990's, a friend of mine was heavily dating potential candidates back to back. She had complained that it was exhausting going out with one guy after another everyday of the week after work. She's currently happily married to the same man for the last ten years. It's one thing to have that one special person you're currently dating, but it's another challenge altogether to find that person to start dating. This requires meeting someone new periodically hoping you will both feel some kind of mutual magical spark that says, "I like this person and want to see them again."

Most of the time you're not so lucky.

When you're a busy professional, it takes effort after another long productive day to meet someone new. You're exhausted and it probably shows. Now you've got to put on the face to meet this new prospect and hopefully impress them and vice versa. This is how you're presenting yourself to someone new hoping to make a lasting impression.

The love market has changed drastically since as it seems to every ten years. The 1990's was the final decade where love and relationships would never be the same again. The technological age took off bringing the masses gained access to computers and cell phones, which later brought about dating websites, social media, and phone apps. There are definite pros to this as well as the cons to consider as there are to most anything. Having all of these fantastic choices around you sounds awesome initially, but humankind has a built in ego, which causes one to wrestle with and vacillate between making decisions that work and ones that backfire. What came out of the technological age post 2000's is that it became easier to find sex than to find love. Love grew to be lacking more than it ever has in Earth's history.

In my past experience, most prospects that approached me would rather get it on, than take the time to get to know one another and then date. Some of the come-ons are anything, but romantic. You might cringe at some of the messages I've received. It's cutting to the chase, removing the exciting foreplay, and with blunt cold detachment saying what they'd like to do me, or what they would like me to do to them.

In the end, I was left bored, disconnected, and more jaded. Viewing it from an aerial view perspective can be depressing that this is what it's come down to. There is a difference between witty creative flirtatious banter as opposed to approaching someone with thoughtless overused fad phrases, "Horny?" How about, "Horned Up?" Any possibility of getting someone into bed is killed instantly with the wrong line.

There are more singles around the world than those in a relationship. Post 2000's was when the shift began to happen. The media, popular culture, and the high accessibility to technology heavily promoted sex instead of love at a rapid rate. The more a pop artist bumped and grinded on stage or in a video wearing little clothing, the more popular they became. Popular culture was feeding and selling sex to the point where it was suddenly boring and unexciting. But after talking to and interviewing countless people, I discovered they all desired a long-term love relationship, but it was constantly evading them. It was difficult to understand as they were independent, good looking, had a great personality, had their own money, we're caring, and compassionate. What was missing?

The main reason all exist is to LOVE. What else did you think you were here for? Is it to work a job? A job that will one day vanish once your run is complete? Jobs are a necessary means of physical survival, but it's not why you're here. One doesn't need to be married to their job to the point where they have no personal life. Hopefully, you find meaningful work that is your passion, but that's not the sole reason you are here. In the end, it's all about love, yet that seems to be a major struggle to achieve for most. Wallowing in perpetual negativity, sadness, hate, bitterness, and deceit is a much better space to live in. This must be the case since the energy saturating the primary masses around the world swim in the epicenter of its toxicity. Notice the continuing noise of the media and social media with all those negative words being darted at one another.

While the challenges to finding love have increased, it's not impossible to find that one person for life who desires what you want with you. Attracting in a suitable romantic partner entails loving yourself like nobody's business and believing in all that you are. Confidence is one of the key traits that attracts in others to your light and overall essence and energy. This doesn't mean you won't be attracting all sorts of prospects from all avenues, even from those who are not looking for something serious. It includes those unwanted proposals that see you primarily as a piece of meat to help them get off. You have to weed out a great deal of people on the hunt for love. The potential partner is the needle in the haystack and the diamond in the rough that stands out. The majority of prospects seem to only be interested in sex rather than forming a soul mate love connection with someone.

Those in healthy long term love relationships report to being happier, calmer, more motivated, and less stressed in their life in general than those who are single. Note the word, "healthy", because being in a drama ridden love relationship, or unrequited one sided love connection, is just as bad on your health than being addicted to a toxic substance. You might as well be single and develop a healthy social life instead.

Long term love relationships between two people

facing in the same direction that have each other's backs tend to be less depressed, have less anxiety, and lowered blood pressure than those struggling alone with no social support system or a love partner for life. The loving soul connection motivates both parties to accomplish more in their life. They tend to live longer happier lives, rather than short miserable ones. The immense benefits in a healthy long-term love relationship are endless. There is no telling what both partners can accomplish while in a loving partnership.

This is not intended to imply that in order to be happy that everyone should jump into a long-term love relationship. There are some people who are not cut out for it, are not ready for it, or they genuinely prefer to be alone and single by choice. They are perfectly happy being single.

It is unwise to jump into a love relationship when you're not in the right space to be in one. It is also not fair to the person you're pushing to get involved with when you're not ready. If they're pushing you and you're not ready, it is reckless to go along with it knowing that they want what you do not want.

To an extent, realizing your dreams first before getting into a love relationship is ideal, but if you wait for that to happen, then you might be waiting forever. The right partnership gives you that push to conquer your goals by giving you the space and freedom to explore your dreams. Without love within or without, one's talents and accomplishments mean nothing. Love is the reason all are here bridging souls in one long thread of interconnectedness.

When an entertainer receives an award, nine times out of ten they mostly include their love mate in the speech. Some even go as far to say how much their mates love is instrumental. Their lover's immense loyalty and support means the world to them. This is because they are aware of how the person closest to them has been their biggest support system and fan than any other. It's a stronger love than any fan because it's personal. This love partner knows who they truly are behind closed doors rather than the persona that the public thinks of them to be like.

Live life for you with just enough room for another loving soul to merge in with you.

Giving up on love is understandable and certainly not uncommon. Many have protested they've hit a point where they announce that love might not be in the cards for them. They've reached a place where they accept that. It's been years and all they have witnessed is one loveless situation after another. I came across someone who had gone ten years without ever having dated, and then out of nowhere met someone they fell in love with and ended up getting married, so love can happen when you least expect it.

Everyone is having a difficult time where love relationships are concerned because you've got half the world desiring a love relationship and the other half wanting to be free. The best freedom in the world is when you're in the right love connection with someone who gets you and supports you, while you give that to them in return.

You have more people than ever operating from the selfish ego. There is no room for another person when you're in that space. You're expecting the most perfect love partner to enter the picture that bows down and caters to all of your needs. I often hear others tell me what they will only accept in a partnership. It's this long list of outlandish requests, which limits the possibility of inviting in the right person.

Desiring a love partner is not co-dependent. The human soul desires the company of other human souls, even if it's just one person in a companionship setting. This is why many support groups consider solitary confinement to be inhumane. If you were deserted on an island, no matter how much you love yourself you would start to go crazy after a while. This is despite those who are independent and prefer to be alone. I've come across quite a number of people who prefer a solitary life, but even they have those moments where they are surfacing and desiring some attention from another on occasion. To equate a basic human need with desperation is absurd.

Some people have better emotional endurance when it comes to being alone. There are also many people who do not cope well with loneliness. Some of them resort to suicide, while others resort to drugs, alcohol, or sexual promiscuity.

Studies have also indicated that infants who do not receive touch in orphanages have a higher mortality rate. The same goes for senior citizens in care homes. This evidence suggests that human souls need both friendships and camaraderie, not to mention love and intimacy companionship.

Love will not magically appear. You do the work by focusing on hobbies you enjoy and self-improvement activities, but this still leaves you wondering if a love partnership will ever happen. Love circumstances happen when you least expect it. When you fixate harshly on it coming about, then it delays and frustrates the love from entering the picture. All of my serious love relationships came about when I wasn't expecting it or looking for it. Each partner showed up out of nowhere and then the union was driven in full speed motion. Incidentally, I've reviewed cases where those who were happy and single and not interested in a love relationship were the ones who effortlessly ended up in a love relationship. When you let go of the need to be in a relationship, the closer you are to being in one.

CHAPTER THREE

LOOKING FOR LOVE
IN ALL THE WRONG PLACES

Some cultures still prefer on deciding within the family unit who they think you should marry, but this is imposing your free will on another. Love cannot be rushed or forced, and nor can it have burdens placed on its back such as having someone else decide for you. Get to know someone gradually first before jumping into marriage or a committed relationship with someone you don't know.

Consciously searching for a love partner rarely works. There are cases where someone has deliberately raced out and nabbed the person they want to marry and it's worked out, but generally you cannot push or force someone to be with you. It will only be met with resistance and disappointment. During the rare times this has worked is because both people were physically attracted to one another.

A connection based on lust does not always go the distance. A physical attraction is connected to a lust attraction, because you don't know this person well enough to be in love with them. The person's physical beauty blinds one to the truth about them. Being attracted to one's exterior does not guarantee personality chemistry. Eventually the lust filled physical attraction begins to wane if there aren't common interests, communication styles, and similarities between one another. The connections that began as a one-night stand or a physical attraction that have stood the test of time were because both partners had similar interests, values, and communication styles outside of that.

Attempting to rigorously find a love partner generally results in disappointment. I've had many serious long-term relationships and every single one of them came about naturally and without effort. It was almost as if they fell on my doorstep when I wasn't looking for a relationship. As cliché as it might sound, they were chance encounters where we turned the corner and bumped into one another physically, "Oh! Sorry. Are you alright?"

Dialogue happens and the communication sifts effortlessly and excitedly back and forth. Boom! The connection is made and phone numbers are exchanged.

I wasn't actively looking for a love relationship or waiting for one when all of my past partners showed up in the form of a dating or a love relationship. We bumped into one another randomly, or they discovered me through other avenues. Our communication began to build into something more over the course of many months.

I haven't run into any cases where someone was deliberately searching for a love relationship and then it came to them, but at the same time putting in an effort is better than sitting on your couch waiting for your next soul mate to ring your doorbell. Love connections happen when you least expect them to. They can never be forced. When you expect a love relationship to happen, then that prevents, delays, and blocks it from happening. It also creates frustration energy, which pushes it further away from you.

Ten years can go by and yet no lover has presented themselves to you. If most of your thoughts during those ten years are expecting this lover wondering when they will surface, then this prevents it from happening. It's one of the many laws of the universe in the way that things come about.

At the same time, you do not necessarily need to be a passive observer putting in zero effort. If you stumble upon someone on social media, or at the gym, the grocery store, or anywhere and they interest you, then smile and say hello. See where that "hello" can go. Even if it goes nowhere, it at least gets your energy out there in a positive way. This would seem like common sense, but you would be surprised how tongue-tied two people can be when they're both attracted to one another. They feel that it's one sided or part of their imagination. They worry that the other person would never be interested in someone like them. They might feel that the person is out of their league. You don't want to spend the rest of your life wondering if something could've formed with a potential mate if only one or the both of you made a move.

Those who are single and struggling to find love want to know if there is some magic secret to attracting in love. Be a good person and allow that to shine outwardly. Optimism attracts in a love partner more than negativity. Both good and bad people attract in potential love partners everyday. Relationship partners have no prejudice when it comes to the type of person it chooses to get involved with. Good people also get involved with bad people. They might ignore the red flags when seeing this new person through the haze of romance. The reality dawns on them as their knee deep in the relationship.

If you like someone, then go on a few dates with them to see how comfortable you feel. It can take a good 3 to 5 dates before you have a good idea what someone is like. Often people meet once and immediately write the person off. A first meeting is never a date, and nor is it enough time to get to the heart of the person. You have to take into account that on a first meeting people are either distant due to a shy guardedness, or they're extra outgoing to impress. There is some measure of withholding to a degree because most people don't typically divulge the dark sides of themselves to a stranger they're meeting for the first time. A first meeting is not enough time to get to know what someone is like. The exception is someone with strong degrees of psychic sensitivity where they are an impeccable judge of one's character.

If it's an app or online date, then someone might rule a potential out because they're not exactly what they imagined them to be from their pictures. As superficial as it is to base talking to someone based on what they look like, most everyone does it including the ones that are deeper than that. Photos are now touched up and improved to the point that the person looks as if they jumped out of a hot swimsuit model magazine. It's best to have it in mind that most of the time not everyone looks as good as their photos, so expect that to be the case with whoever you meet. When you walk in not expecting much, then you end up being pleasantly surprised. You walk in with an open mind, reserving all judgment and expectations. You're going to hang out and keep it super casual in getting to know them as a friend first.

Keep an open mind and give others a chance to allow something to build. This means they may start off distant with you, but then gradually begin to open up as time progresses on future dates.

If you're single and desiring a love partner, then coming into contact with the right person will come about at the right time. When you have faith that it will, then you have a stronger belief system in place that all things happen for a reason. It is common for one to have some measure of hope and faith on some level and yet still feel as if your faith is waning. Ask for continued assistance and guidance from your Spirit team on what you desire. If it appears that the person you're asking for seems to not be in the cards, then ask for signs if this is the case. Sometimes you might feel you're ready, but you haven't reached that place of being ready for the kind of person your team wants to bring you.

CHAPTER FOUR

TECHNOLOGICAL DATING
– PART 1

$\mathcal{M}$y generation was the beginning of the transition to where people preferred texting over calling someone. I've dated countless amounts of others of all ages. This includes those in their 20's and 30's. I mention that age bracket specifically because I found texting to be the #1 sole primary means of communication for those under forty. While the rest have been naturally moving in that direction since there isn't much of a choice.

Those who were under thirty-five years old between the years of 2000-2015 were the generation that needed to make the transition over to texting as the chief way one communicates with another. They will also be the first to age decades into their senior years watching those they know on social media also age into their senior years and pass on. By the time they reach their senior years, they will have been around those they don't know in person long enough on social media to have a strong connection with them as if they are family. When those around them pass on, then it will have an interesting effect as if it is a close loved one.

Others have complained that they will message a potential love interest on an app or on social media who messages them back, but then the person they messaged eventually drops the ball and they never hear from them again. Technology has caused short attention spans to the point where many seem to be uninterested beyond a hello. With dull like enthusiasm they message the next victim only to find the pattern continues indefinitely without success. Those who utilize the primary way of communicating via text or chat messages on an app are rarely able to communicate efficiently on the phone or in person. They're used to short few word sound bites that when they finally meet someone both people end up tongue tied.

A person on the receiving end grows disheartened and frustrated as they spend weeks and at times months trying to get someone they like to show some kind of interest. Pushing for it will not make it happen. If someone is interested and compatible with you, then they will meet you half way. Hounding them will not make them interested, but instead will turn them off if there was any chance to begin with. If they're not that interested, or only half interested, then this will show too. I've heard others say, "I need to keep posting on social media, liking his posts, and putting myself in front of him so that he doesn't forget about me." If someone is going to forget about you that easily and quickly, then is it really worth it putting in that kind of work into what could be a lost cause?

You have to dissolve out hundreds of people to find that one person who is most compatible with you and has a mutual interest. There may be endless choices at your fingertips on a phone app, but the majority of those choices are not the one. Most people on app dating devices are nonchalant and distant in their communication. They might leave brief responses to your lengthy texts or messages. Finding a happy medium and the right balance between putting yourself out there, and not pushing for it is the way to go. The law of detachment is being detached from fear of what the outcome will or will not be.

Into the 2000's and beyond, those over 40 years old and over have said they prefer the phone call, but those under 40 have said that they prefer the text over the phone call. It was around my generation give or take a few years where the transition to text via phone happened. This isn't surprising as I was moving into my twenties while the use of cell phones and computers began to rise over any other means of communication. It started out where people went from calling one another, to emailing, then it eventually disintegrated into texting. You will notice the trajectory as it went from personal to impersonal contact. This late in Earth's evolution should have been more personal, not less.

When I was in my twenties, my serious love partners were older than myself, but then as I moved into my thirties, I noticed they were growing younger and preferred the text over the phone call. I've always been split down the middle and prefer either when it's called for.

The main way that the average person meets someone new at this time in history is through social media, dating sites, and phone apps. Everyone is at the touch of a finger. The plus side to connecting today is that it can happen quickly. The downside is that you're more disposable and just another number or notch on their bedpost.

You can connect with someone instantly who lives minutes from you on a phone app. This doesn't automatically equate to mutual interests, personality, and communication styles. The breakdown to connecting via a technological device can be much more challenging and greater than the plusses. You don't know those you are connecting with even though you think you do by staring at a photo. This luxury can be taken for granted knowing that you can easily block someone you dislike. You willingly move onto the next victim never fully finding a connection after chatting with hundreds of people over the course of several months.

Don't be so quick to write someone off because they're not expressive with the first few messages. The fact that they continue to respond to you should give you some measure of confirmation that they have an interest in you. If they suddenly drop the ball with your exchanges and disappear, then wait a week or so before you message them again to see how they are. If you get the vibe that they're distant again or they don't respond to your messages, then drop them and move on.

The next level of how others meet potential soul mates is at functions, parties, or events. It can also be while hanging out at areas of interest aligned with a hobby, or being introduced by mutual friends, or while you're out and about.

I've dated quite a few people I've bumped into while at the gym. One of them ended up being a long-term relationship. Other ways I met my past love relationships were by being introduced by a mutual friend in a group setting. We weren't set up, but it was a friend introduction that later took off into more over time. Another love relationship started online, one was in a class of mine at college, and one of the other relationships had come across me through a mutual business connection. There are many ways that love relationships can come about. If you examine my relationship history, it reveals there to be varying ways a love relationship can form. There is no one tried and true way, but it's what works best for you. Get yourself seen by others and be open and receptive while keeping some measure of reality in check is best.

The majority of singles interested in a relationship today participate in the online dating route. This might have been considered unusual or rare in 1997, but by the time it was 2007 more people were connecting this way over any other manner. People use the online, social media, or phone app route because they're not having success anywhere else. Or they're busy professionals and don't have the time to meet people any other way. They might be shy and unable to approach people in person, so it's easier to start out by chatting in messages on their phone. It's also convenient as you can connect with people while lounging in bed or sitting on your couch.

Phone dating apps are one of the big ways that people attempt to connect with others. This has its positives and negatives as anything does. The negatives I've discovered is that dating/buddy apps have been turned into sex apps due to the way one treats another as a throwaway.

I've hung out in areas that I normally would not be attracted to for research. The many that came across me in some of these locales had pointed out they were stunned to find me more or less slumming it in places that didn't seem to fit my personality. They all said I seemed to have a rare quality that was lacking on the apps I was hanging out in and that I more or less stood out because of that. They soon understood when I informed them that it was for research. This is in the way a method actor dives into a role by doing the things the character would do. In the end, I made a number of long-term friendships, which is also not highly unusual in my line of work to become close with my subjects. Didn't you see *Basic Instinct*? This is the writer who ends up taking their subjects home with them in some cases. Many of them are aware that they're messaging clones and that they're just not having any success. They suddenly find that rare bird who stands out from the others and wonder what you are doing in places that would seem beneath you on a regular day.

The dating/sex app is enticing because you log on and suddenly you have endless choices of profile photos to choose from. When I first tried it out and posted up a real profile, I was messaged by hundreds of different people in one day. It can feel dangerously overwhelming and to some maybe even an ego booster. Who would be turned off by so much attention? This is how it can get precarious as you can easily become prey to that deception and grow a big head. When conducting your life in day-to-day reality, hundreds of people are not approaching you in one day to say something complimentary to you. The exception is if you're a celebrity or a public personality. For some, living on a phone app gives them the illusion they are as big as a celebrity with all of the compliments darting at them especially if they're easy on the eyes. Being physically attractive, cute, or beautiful is not an accomplishment.

I'd log onto one of the apps to find another string of nude photos being sent to me without so much as a hello. Some of them cutting right to the chase, "horny?" I'd mumble, "Why are there are so many sluts on this thing?" While I'm no prude, it is a turn off especially since it's the gray matter that appeals to me first. I'd ignore the messages or humor them with no intention of ever meeting to find out how they operate. I'd wonder if that method worked for them by immediately sending a random stranger your nude pics. The person on the receiving end didn't ask for any, but that's how you introduce yourself to them. Perhaps I'm an isolated case, but I've heard many other similar stories.

When you have dozens of these messages a day for months and years, it grows less exciting, especially if you're someone who values intelligence, substance, communication skills, and personality over anything else. These are ironically qualities a boss looks for when interviewing potential job candidates. It makes you wonder what kind of jobs do these other people have, if any? Because it seems unlikely they'd be able to get anything substantial if this is how they are in the real world.

What became disheartening on many of the alleged dating apps was that I noticed about 85% of the people contacting me were only interested in getting it on physically. It's no wonder no one wants the hassle of a relationship as they call it, when they can easily log online and connect to have sex with anybody and then dispose of them. This isn't to criticize anyone who is only interested in sex, but many of the ones only wanting sex are finding their ways onto dating apps that are not designed for that. It takes much more than that to get the attention of a quality person, even for sex. Those only looking for sex are not looking for quality. If you're physically attractive to them, then they will hound you until the ends of the Earth with their nude pics and sexual come-ons until you finally say no thank you. Politely refusing doesn't work either as they see that as attention you're giving them.

There are candidates who send you one or two messages and quickly ask if you're available to meet, which is a waste of time and can be disastrous. This is because you didn't take the time to get to know them. Instead you jumped the gun to meet up only to discover you have zero chemistry with this person. Exchanging few worded banter about nothing doesn't tell you if this is someone you'll get along with in person. Now you've both wasted each other's time.

If you're a busy professional who works full time, you likely would not be meeting people right away after chatting for an hour. The only people who do are those who have quite a bit of time on their hands. They might be the bored sloth lacking in motivation. What kind of connection do you think someone like that will get? A hook up is the best that can come out of that kind of a meeting. If that's what you're looking for, then you've struck gold! Indulging in a hook up while single will not block the right one from entering the picture. Spiritually you must also be careful who you choose to emerge with if even for a one-night stand because you absorb that other person's energy.

This is why many of those candidates remain on dating apps permanently for years chatting with hundreds of people and getting nowhere. The conversations are not anything to write home about since they lack in depth. Most of those particular users I discovered had a vocabulary of six words. You'd have better luck in a prison. This isn't surprising that meeting this person turns out to be a disappointment. They're unable to carry a conversation or couldn't be any more disinterested in what you have to say after you meet. How are you going to meet and talk if you can't text a message on the phone? This is people of all ages too. You expect it from a 20-year-old, but someone who is 47 years old is unacceptable. Everyone wants to meet without talking.

The majority of people out there on apps and dating sites are mostly only interested in hooking up. This is Straight, Gay, Male, Female, Bi, you name it and I tested it out. There are a small percentage of people looking for something lasting, as I heard from them too, but they sadly seemed to be in the minority.

People grow hooked on those they're chatting, texting, or phoning with, but until you've met in person face to face, you are not in a relationship. There are always exceptions, but this can be said about anything that exists. Everyone feels they're the exception, until the connection falls apart. There is no relationship until you've met in person. If you have not met in person, then you are not in a relationship. I've witnessed many cases where others fall into this trap repeatedly only to have it end in heartbreak.

Before you meet in person for the first time, you are getting to know one another. It doesn't matter how often you have texted or spoken on the phone. All of that is thrown out the window until you meet in person. Others grow way too attached, hot, and heavy with someone virtually and by phone before meeting in person. Then they meet in person and it starts to deteriorate after that and they don't understand why. When you are detached about your online dalliance and have no expectations, then you have a greater chance of it turning into a success. You cannot efficiently call it a love relationship until you've spent time together in person.

One reader asked me something I've heard from many people out in the dating field, "Don't you think that's weird that I finally met this person, and then afterwards he's suddenly busy with work? I hardly hear from him anymore, when before we met he had been texting me for two weeks straight practically every second."

The guy is unlikely busy with work all of a sudden. He met you in person for the first time and the reality sunk in that you are not what he had built up in his mind for you to be. This is why you have to protect yourself and not take it too seriously before you've met. You may have texted one another obsessively every single day before meeting, but after you've both met, this either dies down, or dwindles away. Texting or chatting with someone you don't know doesn't automatically translate to success in person. It's not always a lack of physical attraction in person that is not present. It can also be personality, overall chemistry, or a feeling one gets in person with someone else.

Whether one wants to admit it or not, people are particularly shallow. They may see dozens of photos of you, but then when they meet you in person they discover you don't look exactly like your photos or you might look like your photos, but they're no longer feeling it personally. Other cases might have some measure of deceit at play, but the greater deceit is if you're fifty-four, but still using photos from when you were twenty-four. Yes, they exist and I've heard those cases from others as well too.

Keep in mind that no matter how attractive someone appears in their photos that it is rare that the person will look as good or better than they do in their pics. And regardless of how physically attractive someone is or is not to you, if there is no intellectual compatibility or similar values and interests, then it won't move beyond a first meeting anyway.

The first thing people see online, on social media, and on apps is a person's photo. This is the initial selling point on these devices. In that sense, everyone is a marketing guru by marketing themselves online. When advertisers want to run their ads in front of a certain market, they dream up ways of how the ad should look that is enticing enough to get someone to click on it. The same concept is how the world is selling themselves on technological devices. There are so many filters, Photoshop enhancements, and other programs that people use to improve a photo that can be touched up in order to look as good as they can in the pic. Have some measure of reality in check if you're judging someone by how you think they look or how you think they will look in person. Go into it with the understanding that not everyone looks as good as their photos. Someone would be lying if they didn't say they were talking to that guy or gal because he/she is a hottie in their pics. You're going to be disappointed if you're only agreeing to meet someone because of their pics. Photos are an illusion to a good extent. They are a sliver in time captured permanently in a still visual at that particular second, but it's not who they are.

Those new to dating reveal a sense of urgency with

you before you've met them. They bypass the phone conversation, texting, or email and want to take it from phone app chatting to meeting immediately. If you're a busy professional, then you understand that your time is valuable. To spend what little free time you have available jumping from an app to meeting quickly can be draining on your time and energy.

The steps to successfully connecting with someone online or phone app are:

- App Chat/Social Media
- Email/Text
- Phone conversation(s)
- Meet in person

CHAPTER FIVE

TECHNOLOGICAL DATING
- PART 2

*Y*ou're taking time building a connection with someone regardless if it moves into a friendship, dating scenario, or a love relationship. You're not speeding through it since there is no rush when it comes to love.

Online dating websites began their rise around 1995. This gave more serious romantic seekers an avenue to meet people outside of bars or online chat rooms. By the early 2000's, online dating websites were super popular and quite common. Around 2010, the phone apps began to rise beyond the online dating website route even though online dating websites continued to reveal success for some candidates. Around the same time social media started to grow and pop up in large numbers as the years progressed beyond 2010. This gave people another efficient way to quickly connect with others. Over the years, I've come into contact with some of the most incredible people through social media, some of who have been loyal readers of my books and me personally, and I'm not an easy person to get close to or talk to for that matter, but some have been able to do it.

Everyone is creating an app for someone's phone to the point where there are eons of choices. Some of the other challenges is it crumbles relationships of all types from love to friendships. You know you have an addiction when you'd rather sit on your phone sifting through the latest profiles on an app rather than develop or fix the connections you currently have.

Those looking to seriously date started to move away from online dating sites as they found connecting with others through the means of networking on social media was becoming more successful. To one extent, they didn't really have a choice, as the pickings grew slim on the online dating websites since people were transferring over to social media and phone apps. Some companies running online dating websites will insist that those looking for a serious long term relationship will be willing to pay higher prices. The concerns I've heard from others is they've paid the high prices to message no one they were interested in. They were facing the same short attention spanned group they encountered on the dating apps, so they figured may as well as stay on the apps since it's either free or costs far less money than an online dating website. Regardless, endless statistics continue to pop up citing there are more singles than those in relationships than ever before in history, especially in the United States. This points to a greater problem beyond online dating websites, social media, and phone apps to meet others. This has to do with the mentality of the masses as a whole and where the state of humanity is at.

When people get to know someone through these avenues, they easily move onto someone else when they grow bored or learn something minor about them they don't like. There are no perfect people in the world. You open up your app and receive messages from someone who is sending the same message to you and those around you. It's shotgun communication where the ultimate goal is to get you into bed with them. They are randomly communicating with many at the same time juggling all of them hoping one will turn out to be the one, but none of them do. There are only a small percentage of people on the planet who are exceptional when it comes to multi-tasking. They don't drop the ball on anything they're multi-tasking with. The world is ruled by narcissism and that means the more the merrier. Everyone desires endless praise, popularity, and support. They're happy to obtain it from one another, but even the famously wealthy have stated they feel lonely and isolated despite being popular in their entertainment career. The gratification that all are chasing after is a mirage in the end. This is because true happiness is derived from within and not from external outside sources. You may receive endless praise gliding high on this support, but the next day it comes crashing back down if it's not consistent.

A potential candidate would meet me and immediately after our meeting, I would be bombarded with endless texts on a daily basis of how into me they are and how much they miss and love me. Their behavior was more akin to someone who has been in a relationship with you for some time, but this was someone I had met once for a couple of hours. By the end of the week of this texting banter, the ball was finally dropped and never heard from again. On the one hand it's admirable to come across those who are not jaded, but some measure of reality should be in check. Can you imagine if I had emotionally fallen for this play only to discover it ripped away without warning days later for no reason. It was fascinating to watch someone go from 0-80 in ten seconds after one hang out.

The easy accessibility to connecting with anyone around you in your vicinity rose to greater heights with phone dating apps. This gave rise to the ego, which made it feel as if you are a kid going crazy in a candy store wanting more, more, more! The ego doesn't care about quality, but instead focuses on quantity. There is a good deal amount of people who long for a committed love relationship and take who they're communicating with seriously, but statistically I found that the majority do not. Interviewing hundreds of people revealed a common theme. It pointed to massive frustration in being unable to find a love partner or friendships. It's a war between that group and the group who want no emotional attachment with someone they want to sleep with. They want to get off once and then you can go. It's primal and animalistic hitting up one person after another in its vicinity with the word, "Horny? I only have twenty minutes." How is this different from renting a whore? It's cheaper that's for sure. With that said, it is no surprise that the prostitution field took a hit once the sex app came to life. Except that perhaps prostitutes usually know what they're doing once they enter the bedroom. You get what you pay for.

You come into contact with someone new who you feel or sense a mutual magical spark. As you get to know this person over the course of a few weeks, you find that you're no longer feeling much lift off with them. Your heart knows if this is someone you want to continue getting to know and grow close to or not. When you have to question it and wonder what their interest in you is, then it's likely they don't have the same interest as you. This is why you're not changing your profile to *in a relationship*, because you're only *dating* them. Dating is getting to know this other person gradually to discover if there is a connection or a match that lasts a lifetime.

People date because they're looking to see if this other person is long-term relationship material. They're not dating to pass the time. It's dangerous to be dating someone when you have no intention of ever truly committing. This is not having integrity, unless of course you've told the person you're dating that you're not looking for anything serious, and you're just casually dating them. If they've mutually agreed that they are cool with that and want that too, then you have a consented match. There's nothing worse than one person being more interested than the other in a pairing up. I've been on both sides of the spectrum, and perhaps you have experienced it as well. This is either liking someone too much or not liking them enough. This is an imbalanced connection that will inevitably disappoint or hurt someone.

Never consider a first in person meeting a date. When you meet in person, you are meeting for the first time and the rest gets tossed out. Look at the first in person meeting as if you're just meeting the person to hang out with no pressure of anything. It's almost like a job interview, because you are both meeting to gauge whether or not this is someone whose company you want to continue keeping.

A nineteen year old male reader said, "That's really

insightful about the first meeting not being a date. I've always felt nervous pressure when it comes to meeting people for the first time, because I treat it as a date and not as a meet and greet. That being said, what are the most fundamental ways to meet up with someone? Is it as simple as coffee, or a walk in a park?"

A first meeting should never be considered a date because you don't know this person well enough yet. Even if you've been communicating via a technological device, you have not hung out with them in person which is the real test. There is too much pressure associated with an in person first meeting to call it a date. You are too busy wondering if you'll like them and wondering if they'll like you to be concerned about how this alleged date goes. If you both choose to see one another again after that first meeting, then you can call it a date. Expect that most of the time there may not be a second meeting.

Coffee is safe and harmless on a first meeting, but there also isn't anything wrong with getting creative beyond that. This first meeting should be light, fun, and short. This means no more than an hour if both can help it. At least plan before meeting that it'll be no more than an hour. There is nothing worse than one or the both of you are silently displeased at feeling no spark and wondering who will be the one to awkwardly cut it short. When you both agree to the hour or less, then there is no pressure. It's also polite to give one another that time to have a conversation. If both see it as a mutual match, then it'll be felt on both ends, and will end up seeing one another again where you can spend as much time as you like on that real date.

A walk in the park is fantastic for a first meeting, because you're keeping it casual by walking alongside with someone as if you're hanging out with a friend. At some point in this walk, the two people should sit down and face one another. If all you do is go for a walk somewhere, then you're not really looking at one another. You're walking and facing forward for the most part. A face to face connection where both eyes are locking is immensely important to establish a soul connection. This is regardless if it's a union that goes nowhere in the end. Incorporate at least a five to ten minute sit down somewhere with one another. This would also rule out going to see a movie on a first meeting. That would be a poor move to meet some stranger for the first time only to sit next to them in the dark and face forward staring at a screen instead of talking to each other. Speaking of screens, keep your phone turned off during this meeting or at least on vibrate. Avoid using it during this hour unless there is an emergency.

Coffee seems to be the standard default line that others ask when wanting to meet. It couldn't be more cliché or bland. Not everyone drinks coffee, but there are other things on the menu. You're sitting in a busy coffee shop with strangers within ear shot. For those who are super guarded or uncomfortable with chatting it up with a new person amongst strangers listening in, then this can be uncomfortable for them. They may not easily open up, and you want both parties to be able to freely communicate. You may choose to grab the drink and go sit somewhere away from it all with the person or take a stroll with them. If you're in an entertaining area, then this can help with conversation flow by pointing interesting stuff out along your walk.

The biggest line I've heard others say with someone they want meet in person is, "Would you be interested in meeting for coffee or a beer?"

Introducing alcohol into the mix is an iffy request. Not everyone drinks alcohol. Those that do drink socially or casually may not want to consider that for a first meeting. Having one drink takes the nervousness edge off, yet judgments are impaired to the point where you're not truly getting to know this new person. You're getting buzzed where everything seems great, but what happens when that buzz wears off? One or the both of you realize you don't recall much from this meeting or your perception has shifted where you don't feel as exciting about them as you did while high on alcohol. If alcohol is introduced, then keep it to one drink for an hour and then wrap the meeting up.

Other considerations should be taken into account when meeting for the first time is that some prefer to meet in a crowded safe place. This is specifically for women who need to be cautious if they don't know who they're truly meeting. You'll want at least one close friend around you to know about this meeting.

I was with someone romantically who said after we met that I was the one they have chosen to hire to date and that they won't be meeting with anymore applicants.

When you meet for the first time, you're secretly looking to see if it's a potential match, marriage partner, date, or even friendship. When there are more meetings or regular conversations with the person after that, then you know that you both like each other enough to get together. You soon start to get a sense over time as to how you want to define the connection. This is whether it's a friendship or if it's a more serious relationship potential, dating, friends, friends with benefits, or the l'amour kind of love.

Love is something that takes time to happen and build. If you're immediately in love with them after you meet them for the first time, then you're not in love, but in lust. There's no way you can love someone you don't know in a deep way. If you've been with them a year and you know their quirks, flaws, challenges, and yet you still love them, then it is real love.

I went on a first date with someone who said, "You're cute, will you be my boyfriend?" I kind of pulled back, "You don't know me." My Casanova candidate said, "So." Well, I guess that solidifies it then.

Needless to say, this wasn't a connection that went anywhere. If it starts off that superficially naive, then there is little chance of progress to something long term. You cannot efficiently get to know someone well enough without spending a good deal of time with them in person.

I've received cases from people who live in one country and are pining over someone in another country. They believe this connection is the one until the one they have their eye on communicates with them less, and then abruptly backs out.

Until you've met in person, try not to take it too seriously. The odds of it ending in disappointment are high. You'll begin to know if it's something substantial if you both find that after you've met that you're communicating even more than you had before you met. You've also gone out with them several more times. In today's dating market, people are lucky if they get a second date with someone they were communicating with online or a phone app.

After about three to five in-person dates minimum

you begin to have a better knowledge of how you think it's going to go. You understand what their basic nature is like, what some of their interests are, and if it's compatible with yours. You spend the next three to six months in the honeymoon phase. This consists of growing closer and developing a routine with one another.

Many run into issues by the six-month mark and leave the connection. They make their exit because they realize they do not like the routine of being with the same person day in and day out. They've become familiar enough with this new person that they've grown bored with them. This is a society built on instant gratification and then they quickly jump cut to something or someone else. If someone doesn't like something, they leave instead of looking for ways to work it out or compromise. If you refuse to compromise, because you've got a large ego, then you'll end up alone. Take the time and get to know someone before jumping in. You can't make anyone do what they don't want to do or what you want them to do. This goes for anything and anyone. Stop trying to control others to be what you want them to be.

Social media and the dating/sex app has killed many relationships. Before email and texting was the norm, you had to face the person to ask how their day was because you didn't know how it was. You're not seeing them all day. Before texting, you had to call the person to talk to them. Today you're considered a rare individual if you're on the phone with someone talking. Wow, what a concept!

The younger my suitors were, the less likely they were to get on the phone and talk with me. I received more texts from them than actual phone calls. Before technological dating, if you were involved with someone you had to take action to connect, which meant calling or driving to see them. Now that there is an ease in communicating or connecting with others, it's also created an aloof distance.

Connecting with someone physically is out of this world. This includes kissing, touching, cuddling, holding hands, looking into each other's eyes, and connecting with one another's soul when you communicate. Having no physical connection with a partner is a sure way to slowly kill the union.

Social media, apps, and popular culture have contributed to killing long term relationships. There is pressure to be unrealistically perfect especially on the outside. Everyone is looking for that physically perfect Adonis that looks as if they popped out of a hot magazine, some of which are fake profiles.

Beware of fake profiles or spam accounts. A couple of ways to tell it's fake is if the profile has a maximum of 1-2 photos on it. Those who are serious about connecting with someone will put up an average of four to five photos or more if the site or app allows. If someone is beyond good looking or appears to be an airbrushed model messaging you, then you'll want to be leery of that. If you're always being hit up by good looking people that's one thing, but if they are super out of this world good looking, with one photo on their profile, and there is little to no realistic information on their profile, then it's likely you're being hit up by a fake profile or spam. If anyone messaging you sounds too good to be true, then that's because they are likely not real. Trust your instincts if someone writing to you feels off.

You'll know for sure with these signs:

- The messages they write are inconsistent from one another.
- They don't seem to answer your questions.
- They only have one to a few photos available with no more to provide.
- The few if any photos they have are of someone way too good looking almost like a model.
- They don't seem to be reachable other than by email.
- They ultimately ask you for money by giving you a sad story about how they're unable to get the money themselves because of some outlandish roadblocks. If someone has 4 million dollars, they're not going to ask a stranger for their bank account information.
- The other way is they end up sending you a link to see more photos of them. Don't click on that.

One popular app at this time is called Tinder. It is for everybody of all ages regardless if you're straight, gay, bi, male, or female. It presents you with one photo after another where you swipe right on the photo if you like what you see, and you swipe left if you don't. If the person is attractive to you, you're swiping right, if not, then you're swiping left. Look at how many you're doing that with and what the end result is. Some choose to keep it contained by only allowing a few matches, but let's face it; most I've run into have informed me that they are gaining more than a hundred matches. I know because while I was doing research on it, I gained over nine hundred matches that were almost pointless to have since nothing much came out of that. Keep the mantra of seeking out quality over quantity. The reason I was doing it was for study. To see what benefit it was to having that many candidates who chose to match with you. What was the benefit? Absolutely nothing.

Speaking of benefits, one of the luxuries of Tinder is that you can choose who you match with. No one is able to message you unless it is a mutual match, yet having a mutual match doesn't automatically equate to a mutual match. One may match because you are physically appealing, but that doesn't make one a match. I ran tests where I would initiate contact with who I matched with, then I ran another period of tests where I would see who would initiate contact with me. When I initiated contact, I hit every single candidate up. About 90% were great at responding back...at least once. Only about 5% of them continued the dialogue communication after that. The rest of them remained matched with me long after they dropped the ball in the communication. Most of them were unable to carry a conversation beyond, "Hello. How are you?"

They were unable to articulate anything about their day. I couldn't imagine they would end up with a lifelong friendship or a love relationship with someone considering they were unable to communicate beyond a few words at a time. In many respects, technology has rendered people incapable of truly connecting and communicating. I wondered what all generations were learning in the education system, because basic human etiquette was definitely not on the curriculum. This is also why I've always insisted that the education system include basic human spiritually based classes in learning how to function in society with others using compassion and awareness. The current mandatory education lessons do not work.

After listening to others stories, I found that I wasn't the only one experiencing this. It was a common complaint that someone had hundreds of matches where the person drops the ball in communicating, but stays matched with you. I like you, but I don't want to talk to you. It certainly didn't personally give me any kind of boost in ego having nine hundred matches. It felt more cluttered than anything else.

One profile said they had over twelve hundred matches and no relationship. I thought that was fascinating, interesting, and telling. About 1% of the matches I made put in equal effort and we're able to carry a conversation. This proved that this person does exist, but you need to sift through hundreds and hundreds to find them.

There is also something eerily superficial about swiping left and right over a profile photo in front of you. The app includes a space where you can write stuff about you, but another fascinating discovery was that most don't have much filled out about them on there. I found it to be a bland group of people with nothing to say about themselves. Without effort, you can guarantee you'll remain single. Posting your pretty face up in a photo is not going to make any kind of relationship happen. The profiles that were filled out to the max were the rare people who were able to communicate efficiently, but like I said they are in the 1% of gems who are relationship material.

It doesn't matter how good-looking you are if there

is no substance. The majority I found to be lacking in substance. If you're looking for a serious relationship, then you'll want to include hints of the kind of person you are. If you excel in your work life or attract a loyal group of friends that never leave, then this is a good quality to have and points to someone who works at something to make things happen. I've noticed red flags in some profiles where all of their photos show them holding an alcoholic beverage in their hand, or every photo is them with other people. Dating apps are designed in a way for you to promote yourself, not your friends, or that you're a lush. If you're not looking for anything serious with anyone, then there are other apps available for those who are looking for a good time. These are apps such as Pure or Skout for straight sex, and Grindr and Scruff for the gays. Although there has been some debate that others find Tinder to be a sex hook up app for straight people, while Tinder is more of a serious dating app for gays. This reason is that gays already have Grindr and Scruff to use as a hook up app, and have decided to make Tinder for more serious connections.

The apps listed are what is popular at this time. If you find that you're reading this and those apps no longer exist, then this is a sign that they didn't hold up and stand the test of time. Most of these apps have been around for a number of years at press time though. Regardless, there will always be some form of connecting with others for dating, relationships, or sex. These examples can be applied to most any manner that you connect. It'll be interesting to see where Earth's history is at in a hundred years where dating is concerned.

CHAPTER SIX

IN LOVE WITH SOMEONE
I HAVEN'T MET

*K*eep the one you have your eye on who you have not met in person at a neutral level. This is where you ensure they are aware you have interest in them, but you're also realistic and have your head about things. Try and not get hot and heavy until after you meet in person. If it's mutual, then you can drive full speed ahead. Others have written to me in a heavy emotional state where they've grown attached, hot, and heavy over someone they haven't met. They meet in person and it starts to deteriorate after that and they don't understand why.

The best ways to navigate with someone you haven't met is when you both incorporate an equal amount of balance and reality. You keep the connection light and fun without it reaching an emotionally dramatic level where hearts end up broken because one of the two loses interest quickly after meeting. When you are realistic, then you find relationship success!

It's easy to grow hooked on someone you enjoy communicating with through chatting, texting, or phoning. Until you've met in person face to face, you are not in a serious relationship. You cannot have a serious relationship with someone you've never hung out with in person before. There are always exceptions, but exceptions are not observed only generalities. Exceptions can be said about anything that exists, and most everyone feels they are the exception.

You've texted or spoken on the phone with this new online conquest, but as soon as you stand face to face for the first time you are starting from scratch. You might have some background information about them before meeting the same way an employer has seen the resume of a potential candidate they're going to meet with. The resume may have wowed the employer enough to want to meet with them, but it doesn't automatically equate to getting the job. It's only after the employer has sat with the candidate face to face that they are able to truly make a decision whether or not to move forward with them or not. Technological dating is similar in that respect.

Barbara disagrees with the mantra that states until you've met in person, then you're not in a serious relationship.

She said, *"I will have to disagree with the statement about there being no relationship until you've met in person. James is the guy I'm having issues with, but he's a different story. I was involved with James first as friends. After a year of that we moved into being in a relationship. This was all happening before we met. Our connection wasn't just online, but through daily phone calls that would last for hours on end. I don't expect anyone to understand this, but we had a really close bond and a real relationship."*

Note the two keywords that stood out, "issues" and

"had". Why were there issues? And why is it past tense as if it's over?

Barbara viewed her connection with James as being in a serious relationship, even though they hadn't met yet. Two years into this scenario, Barbara finally met James in person. They deteriorated rapidly after that never to hang out in person again beyond that first meeting. She attempted to hang onto the possibility with him over the course of the six months that followed, but soon discovered he was flirting and communicating deeply with another woman. This other woman did not include his ex-wife who he was still living with all throughout his online dalliance and phone calls for hours with Barbara. James failed to mention this shred of information to Barbara during all of those phone calls they had between one another for a year. If you are in an allegedly serious relationship with someone for a year who you haven't met, then you would have discovered that information by that point.

Barbara and James also resided in different countries with an ocean between them and not enough funds to commute. Many want to believe they are the exception to the rule, when nine times out of ten; the rule ends up being accurate. This is in no way intended to degrade what someone has together or to devalue that love. None of it is said as a criticism or to belittle anyone who is in a long distance relationship with someone they haven't met. This is said to protect you and your heart, because in more cases than not, it doesn't always continue on favorably.

There are exceptions such as where Chris and Sabrina developed an online relationship with one another that was similar to Barbara and James. The only difference was that Chris and Sabrina were communicating online and via phone with one another as friends for a couple of years. After they met, they realized there was a magic spark in person and it grew from there. They ended up getting married, moved into together, and had Children.

We've illustrated the two separate circumstances where an online long distance relationship didn't work and another case where it did. The difference was that the couple that sustained the distance kept their connection light and fun without falling into intense seriousness until after they met.

It's easy to develop a close bond with someone you're connecting with online. You start talking to someone who is enjoying their banter with you. You're talking to someone who is listening to all of your worries, stresses, and concerns. You feel appreciated and your feelings start to grow for this person. What is not understandable, advisable, or wise is turning it into a love relationship before spending time in person. It's easy to get attached when you put your faith and heart out there with someone you think you know, but you really don't.

In this particular case, it does not always work out as is evident of the Barbara and James scenario result. When they finally met in person, the connection began its rapid decline afterwards, which only further solidifies the statement that you never want to get that attached to someone you haven't met. Your both fixated on one another's photos along with having someone who is listening to your deepest intimate secrets. It gives the illusion of closeness until you meet in person where it doesn't always move forward beyond that.

Barbara had a love relationship with someone she spent only a handful of hours with in person. She developed a deep love for James and then witnessed what the outcome was in the end. She spent the second year with him as an emotional wreck unable to move forward in life. She was extremely distraught, depressed, saddened, and upset on a weekly and sometimes daily basis. Barbara reached out to strangers, psychic readers, counselors, and anyone she could for answers. They were all enabling her by telling her that the two are meant for each other, but in the end none of that panned out or came to fruition. It ended up in crushing heartbreak.

James was not emotionally attached to Barbara, but instead vented his irritation and frustration he was having with what he perceived to be her emotional outbursts that were layered with demands and ultimatums. You cannot change others to be what you want them to be or do what you want them to do. In the end, Barbara and James merged from a mutual appreciation to an unrequited romance where one was more interested in the relationship than the other.

You cannot have a real relationship with someone who is across the ocean who you have never met. Some might believe they have one with the person they're chatting with because of the perceived technological bond that gives off the illusion of one. It does not become a real relationship until you are spending time together in person physically to see that you have a connection, and then you both take it to the next step, which is a full-fledged love relationship. You can make plans with this person that you hope to meet and be in a relationship with them one day, but until that happens it's just a dream. The connection grows and builds into a long-term committed relationship after you've met.

This isn't to say that relationships that start out online and long distance do not work. On the contrary, there are many successful cases where two people who are now married or in a committed relationship had started out chatting online and by phone for years before meeting. The crucial difference is that all of them stated they kept the connection on a deep friendship level first with the understanding of the potential reality. It was only after they met in person years later that the relationship began to progress into something romantically committed. This is about armoring yourself and taking care of you.

I had a friendship that began as an online, chat, email, and phone connection for two years before meeting. The friendship started out as an acquaintance partnership the first few months, and then gradually moved into a friendship that steadily and naturally moved into a best friendship. This is all without saying a word about romance, no demands, no titles, nothing. After we met in person two years afterwards, then it was full speed ahead for us over the months that followed. It went from best friendship to romantic relationship gradually over the five months following our meeting in person. It would go on indefinitely for years after that.

Solidifying a friendship online with those you haven't met is a different set up, because the heightened emotions are not present. It's easy to have a best friendship with someone online you know through social media or other avenues. One of the benefits to technology is that you get to connect with many wonderful people around the world online without having physically met them.

Your Spirit team would never plant your only potential soul mate in one state and then let you lose out on love because you had to move to an entirely different state. There are many potential soul mates, men and women, who could fulfill you spiritually, emotionally, and physically. They are waiting for you in every city, occupation, and social group you might possibly choose to be in at some point in your life.

I've connected in a strong bond with others who don't live near me. It started out as a long distance connection, but the dynamic was a friendship with a strong bond. We never said that we were in a love relationship. It never got to the point where there was misplaced hysterical emotion over what the other one was doing or not doing.

Once it gets to that hyper emotional place over someone you haven't met, you have to question how far you've idealized this person who is not responsive to your cries, but instead dismisses or blocks you. At that point you come to the reality that the person you're upset over has become an addictive obsession. After you've had a long distance connection with someone and then you meet in person, you'll note if it gradually begins to build into more from that point or if it starts to dissolve. If it builds into more, then you have discussions about eventually moving to the same city as one another. Before that, you keep it realistic and on a friend level.

Taking an online friendship into a deeper connection includes spending a great deal of time with them in person. This entails merging physically, mentally, and emotionally several times a week anywhere from two to ten hours at a time sitting inches away from them. You can have date night once a week where one of you properly picks up the other one and goes out somewhere. You take turns deciding what you'd like to do together where there is agreement. It is vastly different spending time with someone in person than having an online relationship. You're seeing their nervous ticks, reaction shots, behavior, facial expressions, and neurosis. The realness of them comes to the forefront. It's not disguised or masked behind a distant technological device.

Some people tend to bond more emotionally than others, and this can present a problem if the emotional bond grows rapidly for someone you haven't met who has not changed their emotional feelings for you. The challenge is when your emotional feelings grow for this other person, but the other person begins to lose interest.

Cindy wrote that she had been chatting, texting, and phoning this guy daily named Drake. Drake was messaging her every single day for weeks. Cindy grew abruptly close to him in a deep way, and then they met in person. Afterwards, Cindy said Drake stopped messaging her. When she reached out to him to see how he was, she discovered that he always seemed to be busy with work. She didn't understand it as they were getting along amazingly. He wasn't that absorbed in work before they met.

Another case is where Brian and Mark were messaging one another throughout each day until they decided to meet weeks later. After meeting, the texting dwindled and died down until they were no longer communicating. Brian couldn't wrap his mind around what went wrong. It might seem to be common sense and obvious that once the two people met they got a feel for how they really are and one of them lost interest. This confused the other person who remained interested, "But we used to talk all day long everyday up until we met. I just don't understand it."

It would seem to be obvious as to why it died down, but surprisingly it's not. The endless notes I receive on similar cases such as this are plentiful and in abundance. Two people chat all day long everyday, then finally meet and one of them realizes they lost interest in them after meeting. They dwindle away with no explanation leaving the other person confused by it. There should be no confusion. Take the halt of the communication as being a sign that the person realized they were just not that interested in you. As tough love as that sounds, it is the reality. This is the challenge when communicating with someone on an app, social media, or online in some form before meeting.

You see a profile blurb and several photos of someone and are enticed and drawn in. You two start chatting and the banter excitedly moves back and forth because you've both idealized one another before meeting. Then you meet and either you or the both of you discover that neither of you are what you both thought.

Perhaps the other person doesn't look exactly like their pictures, or maybe they do look like their pictures, but the chemistry didn't translate positively in person on a personality level. The personalities are opposing and one of you wants to run for the hills. There can be an endless list of reasons as to why the other person decided not to put in any more effort after meeting, but the key factor here is that they're not interested now that they've met you.

While everyone hopes that it is a mutual match, it

can be an ego blow when one of the two still likes the person after meeting, but the other person realizes they no longer do. If you are in a similar scenario and you meet this other person, but you notice they suddenly pull away or start distancing themselves from you after meeting, then take that as a sign they're not interested. They might be interested in you as a friend, but not a lover, or they might not be interested on any level. This is why you cannot take it too seriously before meeting as much as you might like to with some potentials.

You would be surprised how often I listen to these scenarios being sent to me by others. It leaves them in confusion and I have to more or less spell it out, "It sounds like they're no longer interested." Their ego will say, "Well, then why not be man enough to tell me."

That's not the way the world works. Some people don't want confrontation or are trying to spare your feelings from getting hurt by stating the obvious. They don't owe you anything, because they had no real relationship with you. Having animated and excited text banter for three weeks straight is not a relationship. You're still chatting with a stranger. This goes back to the mantra that until you've met in person, then you don't truly know them. You don't know what they're really like in person with flaws and all. You don't know what their personality is truly like until you're with them in the same room. You don't know their ticks, moods, personality swings, and all of the colorful nuances that bring someone to life in person.

Someone can be extroverted online or via text message, but then you meet them and they're distant, cold, or introverted. It's easy for someone to be extroverted on a technological device because you're hiding behind the protection of a screen. This is why you have to take it light and easy when you start chatting with someone new and not take it too seriously no matter how physically attracted you are to them.

Let's face it, nine times out of ten the only reason you've agreed to start chatting with them to begin with is because after seeing their photos you thought the person is cute, handsome, beautiful, hot, gorgeous, or sexy. Very few people will look at a profile of photos of someone they're not attracted to, but then read their profile and go, "Oh hey, this is someone I'd like to know."

The reality is that most will agree to chat with someone if they feel there is something about the other person they find physically or interestingly attractive first.

CHAPTER SEVEN

CODEPENDENCY

*F*orcing love to happen pushes it further away. It brings up fear that it won't happen and frustration that it isn't happening. This energy turns others off whether it's a potential partner or someone you're dating. It puts stress and strain on a relationship with its intensity of trying to keep the connection going out of an obsession to hold onto them.

The reasons behind this behavioral reaction often have to do with psychological build up from childhood of losing something you wanted whether physically or metaphorically. It can also point to having been denied love growing up, which breeds co-dependence. The other reason is that you've become so excited to have a new love partner that it feels as if you found the one and don't want to lose them. You overcompensate to the point of smothering the other person, or by becoming completely co-dependent that it begins to suffocate them. The other partner ends up retaliating angrily, pulling away, or ending the connection altogether. This could be applied to someone who isn't normally co-dependent by nature. A great deal of independent detached professionals announced that the times they have rare co-dependent feelings rise are only while in a love relationship.

When you become co-dependent on someone, then this can manifest in other negative ways such as inciting panic by frantically fixating on every shred the person does or says and becoming suspicious about it. It's this negativity that can spread into other areas of your life too.

Obsessive codependency is the result of psychological build up that trained the mind to cling tightly to every potential partner that comes your way. To some extent its human nature to cling tightly to someone you have a physical attraction for. Think about how that might come off where you're anxious when you meet someone in hopes that person will succumb to the idea that they will be the one you will try to get into a relationship with because you have a mental deadline.

There was a case where a woman was giving the guy she was dating three months to decide if he was in the connection with her or not. He was unsure in the initial stages of their dating as he was still getting to know her. She required an immediate title in order to feel more secure. Insecurities can tear a potential couple apart. When two people in a connection are at odds as to what they are, then this will kick off future issues. The way to prevent that is to either meet half way and accept the others position, or consider dissolving the union. Putting an expiration date on a connection squeezes out any kind of enjoyment of dating this new person. It's supposed to be enjoyable and fun, not miserable and full of anxiety.

Some people are bathed in heavy emotional drama attempting to blackmail, intimidate, or force the one they like to make a decision as to whether or not they are in this with them or not. This will not make anyone jump up and down wanting to be with you, but will instead turn them off. Connections need room to breathe whether it's dating or a relationship. If you intend on suffocating a love mate, then don't be surprised when they pull away or end up leaving.

When getting to know someone you are investing in time, energy, and money. Emotionally attaching to someone quickly who is the exact opposite of that and prefers to take their time with someone will result in a frustrating match that will meet its demise sooner than later. All of this falls into some form or level of co-dependency.

Co-dependency in a love relationship is deadly. It is when you cannot be apart from your lover for any amount of time or you start to grow insecure or depressed. Relationships need room to breathe and co-dependency can suffocate partnerships depending on the personalities of both. You can also be co-dependent when you have an addiction to unhealthy relationships with anyone, whether it's a lover, friend, or family member.

Love relationships have the biggest probability of reaching co-dependency, because of the deep intense love feelings involved. If the deep love feelings spin out of control and manifest into something negative, then this is where you'll have trouble. Typically, what is manifested is fear, which comes from one's ego. It is fear that your partner will leave you, doesn't love you enough, or doesn't give you the constant attention you desire. This is when the relationship morphs into an unhealthy toxic addiction.

Co-dependency in a relationship is also supporting your partner's toxic habits and vice versa. They might have unhealthy addictions to drugs or alcohol, and yet you go along with it because you love them or you feel like you can save them. Any addiction the other partner partakes in can be destructive. The addiction can be anything unhealthy, but the worst culprits are drugs and alcohol. Making excuses for the addict is enabling them. It doesn't help you or the other person.

The worst scenarios would be where it drives you to the same addiction. If you can't beat them, then join them mentality. I understand what that's like as I was involved with someone who sold drugs when I was twenty-two. I started to partake in hard drugs out of curiosity, then I became addicted to it. When I was no longer interested in it, I continued to do it in order to be on the other person's level. Eventually I dissolved it and my focus on exercise, fitness, and nutrition rose back to the top of the list.

In another relationship, I was with someone who drank alcohol heavily. While I used to drink abnormal amounts of too much alcohol in my early twenties, I reduced that to social drinking by the time I moved into my mid-twenties and onward. I could go months without having a drink or desiring one, then when I was in a love relationship with someone who drank heavily, I found that I would drink whenever they would drink just to be on their level. When we split, my drinking went back to non-existent and infrequently.

An addiction is where you're unable to go a week without partaking in the unhealthy substance. The addict eventually makes choices that poorly affect their relationship and partner. You stay with this person because you love them deeply, yet the relationship is causing you inner turmoil and heartache.

When one is away from their partner for about 4 or 5 days, then some measure of separation anxiety is typical. How you accept and become comfortable with that is the way to navigate through it. Finding activities and hobbies to immerse yourself in will help you establish less dependency and more independence, which is an attractive feature to others.

What is outlandish is a day or two has passed and you're going crazy without having seen or heard from them. Separation anxiety is when one or the both of you begin to feel anxiety and depression like symptoms over not seeing one another after a period of time. This is much like drug, alcohol, or caffeine withdrawal. What is considered to be on the unhealthy side is if one of the partners is gone for a day or two and these symptoms come up immediately every single time. You're moving right back into co-dependency territory and need to work on having some level of independence and a life. Understandable separation anxiety and co-dependence can come upon couples in a long distance relationship, or where one is in the military, on location for business, or at a conference out of town for anything beyond a week or more.

It can be immensely exciting when you finally feel as if you've met the one that could be the next relationship partner. You've been waiting for so long that you don't want to lose this person. You start to overcompensate by bowing down to their every whim, while cutting off parts of your true nature in order to please or appeal to their senses. You can only keep that act going on for so long before the true you is revealed.

When you become too available for someone you started dating, then it can turn the other person off. The connection faces early burn out, and can make you appear too co-dependent, too clingy, and too available. These are all traits that can be a turn off to potential quality suitors. You don't want to give up your dreams and life purpose because you've discovered several months have passed and you've been completely absolved in this new person to the point where you're accomplishing nothing for yourself. The right partnership offers a fluid balance allowing the relationship room to breathe as you both pursue your own interests and hobbies, while still efficiently connecting with each other from time to time.

Clinging too tightly to a relationship where you get upset when they don't text you back right away is insecurity. This will squeeze out any love that exists. Worrying about the label of what you both are in the beginning stages will also kill any potential for a long-term relationship with this person.

Establish what you are at some point, but not in the initial couple of months unless it happens to come out at the same time between one another, or you have a deadline with how long you'll wait for someone to agree to a relationship. This is more guidance for those who are having all sorts of fear based thoughts that the person they're with is not that interested. Someone can be interested in you, but not the way you desire them to be. At the same time, you don't want to be dating this person for six months and then you discover they've been dating other people while dating you. The labels are merely to give you both an understanding of how you view your partnership. When it's mutually agreed upon, then this is a good sign you're heading in the right direction.

Those who are serious about long-term relationships and building a life with someone are looking for a partner who functions much like a strong business partner. You want someone who can take care of themselves, who is independent, has their own life, and goals. Someone who is self-sufficient in their life is a strong candidate for someone looking for a long-term relationship partner. Don't be distant, aloof, and cold either. You may be busy with projects and work, yet you're still responsive to your mate over anyone else.

This isn't to squash every life out of the love you're building, but it is the reality. The definition of marriage in the eyes of many laws is legally binding the two people together. In many countries this applies to those of the same gender deciding to marry. It's a business agreement whether someone sees it that way or not. When divorce enters the equation, then it can introduce messy court dates and sometimes lawsuits arise. The dividing of assets according to the law is evident. Divorce is one of the top three most stressful events for many human souls. When it is a serious love break up, then the emotional anxiety quotient is as high as someone going through a divorce.

I've been in co-dependent connections where I'm the co-dependent one, and in other cases the other partner is. The occasions where I was co-dependent in my serious relationships were when I was in my teens and twenties. This is not surprising as you are more insecure and not the greatest judge of character during your teens and twenties than any other age. It didn't stop me and I discovered the hard way that this method doesn't work. When you're in the right reciprocated connection there is minimal to no co-dependency.

I've also received cases from others who displayed co-dependency traits with a love partner or a potential partner. They are over emotional, in tears, erratic, and unhappy, yet they refuse to leave the person that is the result of this co-dependency. This prolongs the inevitable ending of the connection that more often than not disintegrates eventually. Either the one who is co-dependent ends it because the person they're pining over isn't bowing and catering to their emotional needs, or the one on the receiving end becomes so turned off and suffocated by it that they end up leaving. Take it easy in a love connection as there's no reason to place unnecessary strain on the relationship due to insecurities. Insecurities are brought upon by inner unfounded phobias, which most of the time are never based in truth. The mind is a clever little thing when the darkness of ego gets involved. It is one Hell of a convincer allowing you to believe something that is not true. Look at how easily the masses believe a news story fed to them that later turns out to have been exaggerated or fabricated gossip.

Avoid spending every mind-numbing minute during the initial dating stages with a new partner. Whenever two people are coming together for the first time romantically, then this can be immensely joyful and exciting for the both of them. You'll be tempted to be with one another all day everyday whenever possible to capture that repeated joy. Work on reining it in and not jumping the gun of spending every waking hour together. Doing so will dissolve all mystery sooner than later. You want your partner to miss and desire you. They won't experience that when they're seeing and hearing from you 24/7.

Keep a good balance of doing things independently from one another while coming together to hang out on occasion. Too often when someone is in a new relationship, their friends never hear from them. They stop getting together with their friends and spend all of their time with their new mate. Months later, the love partnership experiences early burn out and concludes. If the one you're dating is the one, then they're not going anywhere. You'll have plenty of time to have date night later in the week. It'll also make the date more exciting due to not having seen one another in awhile.

CHAPTER EIGHT

THE EXES:
SHOULD I STAY OR SHOULD I GO

*H*olding onto an ex or past lover can prevent you from moving forward with someone new. The deep emotional attachment to a past love would need to be resolved in your heart. By hanging onto an ex, your energy holds onto them, even if they have moved on. There is no room for a fresh and potentially brighter prospect to enter the picture. This isn't to say that potentials won't show up for you, but when your thoughts are heavily on someone else, then this can distract you from the new person that shows up. You may not notice this new person enough to move forward with them. If the new potential has a high vibration and keen sensitivity, then they will pick up on this distraction and the wall around you.

You can still love your ex, but it's the intense feelings that would need to be tempered where your thoughts are not always surrounding them, and what they're doing, or who they're with. You can't find a way to suddenly develop strong feelings for someone new you just met when you're hung up on a past love.

When you develop strong feelings for someone you've recently met, then this is a combination of lusting after them or falling in love with the idea of them, but it will not necessarily equate to long-term love. True love is developed over time for someone. The more you bond with them and appreciate all aspects of them, then the more love can develop. Take the time and get to know someone before jumping into something serious.

You're on a hamster wheel when you continue to repeat the same patterns that lead nowhere. You continue to attract in the same types of mates or you have no forgiveness in your heart with a past flame. The mate that is the keeper and the one you'll end up with for good is often the one that's different than what you're used to. That is if you can break the karmic cycle of attracting in the same types of mates that add toxicity to your vicinity. Forgive yourself and any past lovers that have caused you ill will. Otherwise these obstructions can prevent a new connection from entering the picture and blossoming out of the dating stages. You cannot force an ex to change and suddenly want you again, since you cannot force anyone to do what they don't want to do. Never wait around for someone who is unsure about you, regardless if that person is intended to come back or not.

Having intense feelings rise within you over an ex that left you is understandable. The end of a relationship can feel like the death of a loved one. This is where you go through the various grieving stages attributed to the emotions within the human condition. Some days are fine and you've moved on, and then other days it's as if you've been hit by a freight train. There is no set time period that it takes someone to move on, but when it's a profound love within a serious relationship that ended, then that can take anywhere from six months to a year minimum. Those who move on within weeks are either using someone else to forget about the past love or they were never that interested in the past love to begin with.

Some want to know why they keep attracting the same types in. Whether it's believed or not, you are attracting those types in. If someone is constantly transforming, changing, and ever evolving, then this will have an effect on your connections. When someone changes and evolves, then this has an effect on the types of people they desire. It's also about accepting that everyone is flawed and making the most of the partners you're given. No one is ever going to be 100% perfect for someone. There will be holes and challenges in any connection.

What if your partner wants out?

There are connections where one or both partners are secretly going back and forth in their mind wondering if they should continue the relationship or not. Maybe they're not cut out for a relationship and it was only while in one that they realized this truth. Or perhaps they have fears that they're with the wrong person. If this is you, then take a step back and notice if you're being too picky. If you find that every person you're with is the problem, then it might be you that needs to do some self-evaluating to pin point why you're attracting in the same types and going along with them.

If someone is thinking thoughts of leaving, then the thoughts alone could potentially end the connection through a self-fulfilling prophecy. There is little convincing that can be done in talking someone into staying in a relationship that they don't know how to be in, or no longer want to be in. You know these people since they're the ones that end up circling you at a later date wanting to come back or wanting to be around you. It was after taking a break away from you and the relationship that made them realize there is no one else better. They had it pretty good while with you. If they stay with you out of guilt, they will start to do things that sabotage the connection. They may act out or be cruel in direct or indirect ways. It also might be you who is the one that falls into that description.

The partner that wants to leave is miserable in the connection, and the other partner is unhappy due to being with someone that is disconnected from the union. They sense their lover's body is in the room with them, but their soul essence is not. When you let the one go who no longer wants to be in a relationship, then you open the door to the possibility of someone awesome who wants what you want. It is rare for a new potential love interest to show up while you are still hung up on the current or previous one.

If you have more good times than bad, then this is a sign that the relationship has what it takes to go the distance. If the reverse is the case where there is more bad than good, then it's time to consider moving on. Enduring an unhealthy volatile connection is taxing on your energy and health. This will age you and present potential health issues just as quickly as enduring a bad break up.

Getting to know someone gradually is investing time, energy, and money into them. When you've put years into that with someone and they abruptly leave when there were no issues, then that can damper your world for awhile.

How will you know if your relationship has served its purpose or if it is at the end of its tenure? If you have to ask, then it's over. Preoccupying oneself over whether or not a relationship has run its course indicates that you've already got one foot out the door. When doubt exists in your mind, then this is what shall come to you. Letting go of anyone or anything means you first let go of it in your heart. Once that happens, then the energy is activated and heads in that direction without you realizing it. This same process is applied to attracting in a love partner. You feel it in your heart that the love partner is already here. Use your imagination and visualize that it is in motion by believing with cheerful might that it is here now.

Leaving a connection is a personal choice that the individual must make. You can come to that conclusion by following your intuition on what feels right or doesn't feel right. If you feel uncomfortable feelings surrounding it, then this is a sign that it's time to move on. You cannot convince a doubter and why would you want to. No one wants to be with someone who isn't quite sure of the good they have.

Are you happy with the one you're in a relationship with? If you are, then you stay. If you've been unhappy for a prolonged period of time with someone, then you dissolve the connection. This is also why being clear minded assists in connecting to your own Spirit team for guidance on what feels right. Ask for assistance on the best course of action that benefits your higher self for all parties involved.

If the question needs to be asked, then the answer is that it's more than likely time to bring it to a close. Wondering whether or not to stay or leave a connection is tainting it with that energy. It can also signify that someone is in the middle of a transition or crossroads. All couples go through periods of up and down regardless of the dynamic. You're going to run into issues with whoever you live with at one time or another. This is regardless if it is a love mate, family member, friend, or roommate. Human beings have a dark ego and can be territorial by nature. When this primal aspect is ruling, then it can cause friction with others at times. One or the both of you will more than likely desire space and alone time on occasion. The relationships that go the distance are the ones that treat one another with respect and know when to give each other space when needed.

Doubts are a lower energy that will erode a love relationship. It's not fair to the other person to drag a relationship on with them when you have no feelings left. Release them from your chokehold of staying in the relationship when you know it's over in your mind. Never allow a connection to continue longer than it should when you're not into it. You owe the other person that much so they can get on with their life with someone else more aligned with them.

If the relationship connection is toxic, then there is no purpose in staying. Some of the things that point to a connection being toxic are if it's bathed in abuse, whether emotional, verbal, or physical. There are addictions or addictive behaviors going on, affairs, non-committal behavior from either party, lack of ongoing support, or both partners have drifted apart and have interests that are no longer compatible or accepted. If any of those traits exist in a relationship, then those are signs that the union's purpose has been served.

If there are no major issues or toxicity, then the

question is if there is enough love for the person to want to stay with them and make it work. If the answer is no, then its purpose has been completed. If one or both parties are unwilling to compromise and make it work, then dissolve the connection.

The purpose has been served when you feel good about walking away understanding the lessons you've gained while in the connection and appreciating the time you had together. It's not fair to stay with someone when you have no love for them. Another dangerous choice that some make is they leave you, but they continue to remain in contact. This causes confusion and enduring heartache especially when you still have feelings for them. In order to extricate your exes energy from your aura, you will have to halt communication or keep a huge distance and barrier up.

The other factor to consider is that the ego will convince you to leave. It'll paint pictures that the grass will be greener with someone else. No one should stay with someone who is unsure about the relationship, and rarely is the grass greener elsewhere.

Another sign that shows a relationship is over is where you're putting in all the work and the other person is not reciprocating it or meeting half way.

No matter how many love experiences gone bad it is worth the risk to open up one's heart to allow love in again, otherwise a missed opportunity can take place. When your heart has been bruised and battered, you subconsciously put up a wall that makes you inaccessible to anyone, even the right one. The warmth is what the right one will be drawn into and not the hostility. It can take a long time after one heart breaking connection has ended before you safely drop that wall of horror to allow someone new in.

I've been the one others have left and I've done the leaving. As hurtful as it is to be left by someone you love, it is better they do it quickly rather than stringing you along forever when they have no interest in being there. There is no easy way to leave someone except to just do it quickly like ripping off a Band-Aid. The sooner you do it, then the sooner the both of you can work to move on.

Forgiveness is one of the toughest lessons and challenges to overcome, especially when it's applied to a lover or an ex. No one wants to forgive being slighted or scorned by anybody. This is particularly potent when it's a lover where the feeling is more intense than any other relationship. Being able to forgive is to love unconditionally.

When it comes to a love partner, one assumes this person has their back. They are merging spiritually, mentally, emotionally, and physically with this person on all levels. It is considered a big deal to give all of oneself in that way. When your life mate cheated on you, or was physically or verbally abusive, then it can be difficult to reach a place of forgiveness, although necessary for you to move on.

You can understand how forgiveness can be a challenging place to get to. Forgiving them isn't letting them off the hook for what they've done, but it is letting you off the hook from continuing to absorb any negativity associated with their actions.

Forgiving for one's own sake is a crucial step, but building up the trust in the person again if one chooses to is no easy feat. If the other person did something dreadful to damage your connection to begin with, then it can make it almost impossible to allow them back in. Even if you did, the lack of trust would remain on your mind wondering if it would happen again. It would take hard work and effort to re-build that trust. It can be difficult, but it's not always impossible depending on the nature of the connection and if growth has taken place with the other person.

CHAPTER NINE

DATING IS A BATTLEFIELD,
BE PREPARED TO GET DIRTY

The top positive qualities that are attractive to potentials are strength, confidence, high self-esteem, independence, passion, and intelligence. When going on a date, never put your best face forward since pretending is seen as deceptive and dodgy. You put on the best face in the beginning in all compartments of one's life from relationships to business opportunities in order to lure someone new in. Eventually who you are comes busting out. All of your red flags and flaws are in plain view. The person you deceived is suddenly questioning who you are, and who you are is a complete stranger.

In the past, I've never put on that pretend face on a date. I walk in and immediately jokingly say, "You do know what you're getting yourself into right? If you don't, it will end in tears."

Pre-1970 it was rare for people to drift apart and break up. Instead they made their relationship work. Everyone supported one another while building solid families and communities. Strong social support systems in a human soul's life help carry that person far. From 1970-2000, human life witnessed the rise of break ups, separations, and divorce. By the time 2000 rolled around it would only sky rocket to an astronomical degree.

The world is suffering where love relationships are concerned. This is an ego based planet that includes ego based pursuits, which have taken precedence over merging a duo in a beautiful long term supporting love relationship. The ego contributed to the downfall of relationships. It's the ego that will jump into a relationship quickly and end it recklessly, or the ego will avoid a connection altogether as it dislikes feeling tied down.

Every human being is complex and this complexity needs to be taken into account when examining a love relationship. What works for one couple will not necessarily work for another. All couples need to have the goal of wanting to make it work with one another. They are realistic in understanding that there will be highs and lows, but there is no out. They will work as a team to fix what needs to be mended. People hate their jobs, but they stay. When they hate their relationships, they leave on a whim without thinking it through. Most of the main pockets of human society prefer that everyone be a clone of themselves from worshipping the same God, to being the same race, the same culture, the same political interests, and so on. Tolerance of anyone who is different or chooses differently is not tolerated by the human ego.

There are couples that run into one another for the first time and there is a mutual passionate intensity that cannot be explained. They know deep inside that they have to be with this person. Nothing will stop them from becoming an item. Others have a more tepid way of connecting in the beginning where it's a slow snail moving friendship and nothing romantic develops or happens for quite some time. They're just hanging out every few weeks with the other person casually, while some days they never hear from one another. Somewhere along the way it gradually builds and increases until they find they're solidifying a stronger commitment, moving in together, or getting married. The journey to this end result varies from one couple to the next.

*W*hat someone looks for in a potential partner can be interestingly complicated. If your request is that the person be exceptionally good looking, then you will be heading down a path of disappointment. When you meet someone on a dating/sex app, or on social media for the first time, then you are sizing each other up based on the photos you see. It's more than the physical appearance, although that is the primary factor that one is looking at even if they don't admit that to someone out loud. This is the case even if they are not typically a shallow person and know that it takes more than looks for a love relationship to work. Still, they want to see if this person is someone they are physically attracted to on some level.

In the end, a physical attraction may be the jumping off point, but that is not what keeps someone there. If there isn't anything else that interests them about the person beyond looks, then the connection will be short lived. You may hook up with this person, but then it fades rather quickly after that. This is why many have complained that they never heard from the person again after a first meeting. Perhaps it's because they slept together on the first meeting. When you sleep together on a first meeting, then this is a hook up. Most have admitted that when they are truly into someone that they find they are suddenly delaying the sleeping together until at least a minimum of two to four dates or more. That's a sign of deeper interest.

When you're not that interested in someone on an emotional level, then you jump the gun and get it on. This isn't to say that there aren't a great many long-term relationships where the couple slept together on the first meeting, but that it is a rare thing to thrive into a monogamous connection that lasts for decades beyond that. Many singles informed me that they will sleep around and hook up when it's all they can get, but when they are strongly into someone beyond the physical, then they delay the sleeping with that person. They desire to get to know them on a personal level. It is beyond a lust connection even if they are physically attracted to them too.

When you see the date a second time, then that's a positive indicator that there is potential. I wouldn't jump up and down right away, but it's definitely a good sign. Most meet ups don't make it past that first time. The more you end up seeing and hanging out with the person should reveal to you if the connection has promise or not. Other things that one is looking at when they first meet someone is their social status, their interests, communication styles, goals, work life, etc. Someone looking for a long-term relationship is interested in all aspects of you.

They might ask, "How long was your longest relationship?" They're sizing you up as they see you as a potential prime candidate to merge with, but they want to know things about you that might be a red flag to them, or discover traits that indicate promise or similarities.

*M*ichael met Tiffany and raved to his friends over how great it went and how awesome she was, but he added, "...then she pulled a cigarette out of her purse and I won't date a smoker."

You could have reasonable demands of what you won't accept in a potential love partner no matter how attractive they are to you. Keep your list practical and rational, because there will always be something about someone that you won't like. You will have to learn to compromise on certain issues or face being single for good.

If someone's longest relationship is three months, then a serious suitor might frown up on that. They are looking for something long term in the end and could be hesitant to continue further with someone they see as long term relationship challenged. What could save that and give you a shot is if other aspects of you cancel that bit of trivia out.

You could be long-term love relationship oriented and perfectly capable of going the distance, but ended up with a bunch of frogs, or at least with mates that were not suited for you. It wasn't necessarily you who were to blame for the repeated short-lived connections. It can also be a turn on for a potential who believes they will be the mate that lasts a lifetime with you. Keep an open mind that if someone's longest relationship was brief that it does not always have to do with them. They might not have been the one to bail after several months, but it was the ex who left. There are also prospects that were the ones who left every connection they were with after several months. This is why you would like to know why their relationships were short lived and who did the leaving. If they were the ones to leave, why was that?

There is debate on whether to ask someone what kind of job they do on a first date. This is because one's job does not necessarily define you, but it gives one a clue into what takes up a good part of your day. Is someone a lawyer, a receptionist, or a photographer. It can help point to one's passion and interests if they're doing work that is meaningful to them or if it's a job that pays the bills, but they don't necessarily have any lifelong passionate attachment to it. If they had all of the money in the world, would they quit that job is the real question. Someone who loves what they do would do the work for free so the paycheck is not the factor. It's part of their life purpose as they feel a passionate calling to dive into it without monetary compensation. The best of both worlds is receiving monetary compensation for your passion and life purpose work. Asking someone how much money they make a year is offensive, but I've never heard of anyone asking that before on a date. If they did, I can't imagine that the date continued after that point.

I've had potentials say the wrong thing after two days of not hearing from me, "Wow, this really fizzled out."

It's only been two days, not two months.

Another potential also said the wrong thing after only three days of messaging, "It's looking like I'm wasting my time and that you're never going to meet me." When days pass they assume that it's over and decide to end it prematurely. Beware: If something is meant to be, then it's going to happen and will last longer than a week. If someone is in a rush to make a connection happen, then they will be just as rushed to dissolve it.

A year later when I checked back on those people, they still hadn't been in a relationship or acquired any suitable prospects. The potential prospects were chased away after having a stranger place too close for comfort demands on them days into communication. This is a red flag in the eyes of many. The real deal is willing to take their time with you gradually building something solid and lasting.

Some people love the chase. You come across someone who pines after you at full force. As soon as you start coming around and showing attention, they immediately lose interest. This is someone who is interested in the hard to get or the challenging people. Once they obtain them, it's no longer challenging and they lose interest. They are soon off to conquer and capture another victim.

While on a date with someone, avoid talking about an ex or comparing an ex to the current one you're dating. The person you're seeing doesn't want to listen to someone droning on about how great one of their exes was, nor does it look good if you go on about the bad things they did. Avoid doing that in the initial beginning stages of dating. Wait until the connection has grown close enough before comparing exes.

At some point you both may want to discuss exes, since those who are interested in you are curious what your past relationship choices were like and what went wrong or what worked. Of course they will also want to know that they will be the one to break the cycle of unsuccessful past relationships.

*M*y mother met her second husband on Yahoo Personals when the site existed in 2000. This was during a period where the Earthly shift was moving into technological domination. At that point, the only thing I used the Internet for was to check email. Going on a personal dating site was unheard of to me. When she was telling me about another date with someone I said, "You should take someone with you like your sister." She replied, "You get to know the person before you meet. You get a feel for what they're like."

She had been dating online for awhile and then decided she was going to give up and take her profile down. This was when one more potential emailed her. She said to herself, "I'll meet with this one and then I'm done and closing my account."

Ironically, this man ended up being her second husband. They are still married today. She had greater success than some twenty-something year olds. She was 49 at the time when they met, so love relationships can and do happen for those over 40. Not long afterwards my mother and her second husband married in 2001, I discovered that more people were meeting online. Every other person I was talking to at a party or gathering would tell me a story of how they met someone new on the Internet.

This was when the world grew more to functioning solely online. Now it's out of control where face-to-face meetings are nearly obsolete. You chat on an app and people want to meet you that hour for *fun*. This is instead of getting to know you gradually. They haven't figured out that it's not the way to go, and nor do they care. This method is not successful since more people than not are single wondering if it will ever happen for them.

There are those wanting to meet for fun in the sack that have zero interest in forming any kind of deeper connection with one person. The majority are not able to reach that level of intensity.

You have those that desire something meaningful, but will go along with some fun in the sack in order to connect with another person. Deep down they secretly desire one person to unite with for good.

Many are struggling to find and sustain a relationship that outlasts milk. They don't know how to court efficiently and build something substantial with someone that goes the distance. *Courting* and *chivalry* are no longer part of the vocabulary in the modern day dating world. Those two words are associated with compassion and caring. They were words that others once observed for centuries, then as soon as humankind designed a computer the words became outdated.

Many move onto someone else just as quickly as they start up with you. They are soon chatting with other potentials simultaneously. Everyone is a prospect that never gets any lift off. The attention spans of those today are much shorter than they used to be, and boredom sets in by the tenth date. Technology played a major hand at the development of newer generations of souls. It's taught many to use texting and email as the primary method of communicating. Typing a few words into a box is no longer communicating efficiently. Many companies hiring newer generations of people have complained that those candidates are unable to conduct an efficient interview or have adequate in-person conversations with people. This is translated to the personal dating world.

Some will emotionally attach themselves quickly to another who is the exact opposite of themselves. The other person is doing it the right way, which is taking their time with someone. This is a frustrating match unless both parties meet the other half way. If it's the intended mate you're supposed to be with, then they're not going anywhere. When you rush a connection, you tarnish it in the process. When you are with the right person, you both know this is it without guessing. You're both equally in it, loving, giving, and compassionate together.

The union between two people who are intended to merge as one unit will happen naturally and effortlessly. Both partners know without words, struggle, or questioning that they are in the right union. It isn't unrequited or one sided. This is how you know it's the real deal. All internal psychic senses and gifts are awakened and enhanced in one another's presence when you're facing the same direction. You fight each other's causes together even if the cause is not particularly one you're passionate about. You still support your partner with it. This also means there are a great many love partnerships where both observe an opposing spiritual belief, religion, or political affiliation. When you have two mature adults who accept others differences and choices, then a relationship with opposing interests can be even more successful than a connection where the two are exactly the same.

There may come a point in a long-term serious love relationship where you end up meeting your love partner's family, parents, colleagues, or friends. This is one of the larger complaints coming in from people.

You're wondering if your partner's circle will like you. It doesn't matter what they think of you. What matters is your union with your love partner. The inevitable meeting of your partner's friends or family members may come up. Just because your partner gets along with them does not automatically translate to you.

You hear about the stories where no one gets along with their in-laws. This is because this theory tends to be common and true. If you find you don't care about your partner's circle, then chalk it up to, "It's supposed to be like that."

This is where you put on the face of friendly politeness, but you don't have to be besties with your love partner's circle. Chances are you likely won't and if you do end up liking any of them and they like you, then that'll just make for a smoother ride for all involved, but it is rare.

The best way to meet your partner's parents *(or any other part of the clan)* for the first time would be to not have it in a formal setting such as a restaurant. "We're meeting my parents for lunch at the...."

The more appropriate way is to meet them briefly in an informal setting first where it's a, "Hi", "Hello", and "Nice to meet you."

The second time you meet can be a formal meeting. By that time, you have all met one another briefly and it won't feel like walking into an uncomfortable setting while having to chew food and stare at one another awkwardly. Some feel as if they're being silently judged only to report back to the one you're dating. This same concept applies to anyone connected to your love partner, whether that be friendships, colleagues, or other family members.

CHAPTER TEN

THE BALANCE OF MASCULINE AND FEMININE ENERGIES

*W*hen a soul is born into a human body, it has an equal amount of both masculine and feminine traits. A relationship has a brighter chance at success when both partners exude more of one or the other. This has nothing to do with the genders involved. If a girl asks a guy out, then she is the male/masculine energy. When the boy agrees to the date and allows the girl to plan it, then he is the female/feminine energy. It is irrelevant if his overall nature is typically the masculine energy. Masculine/Male energy is the one who initiates, gives, or takes action. The Feminine/Female energy is the one who lets in, receives, or surrenders.

The best scenarios are the couples that have the balance of both energies intertwining. This is by alternating from the masculine to the feminine. Vacillate from being receptive and going along with something (feminine) to the one making the decisions, initiating, and taking action (male).

If the relationship connection is a partnership where you're both the same gender such as two males or two females, then this still applies. One of you needs to be the masculine energy while the other is the feminine energy in order to create a balance within the duo. This is about energy and not the gender.

If you have two people exuding masculine energies in the connection, then they might experience some level of discord, arguments, or conflict. If you have two people in the relationship exuding feminine energies in the connection, then nothing gets done and no one asks anyone out. There is no movement and no nothing. You need to have an initiator and a receiver.

The best of both worlds is where you are alternating between both throughout the course and duration of the connection. When one of the partners is always initiating (masculine), then they risk growing frustrated as if they're the one doing all the work. There are cases where one partner initiates and as soon as the other partner finally initiates too, then their mate rejects that initiation. This is because they're both in the masculine role.

When a woman contacts or messages the guy she's interested in to make arrangements to meet, then she is now exuding the masculine energy. It will not work if he does not move into the feminine energy as the receiver who accepts her offer. If he's typically used to being the masculine energy, then he will be turned off by a romantic interest being the initiator. If two people have a romantic interest in one another, and they're both sitting around waiting for the other to make a move by calling, texting, or emailing, then they are both the feminine energy. What do you think happens in that instance? Nothing. They will wait an eternity for the other to initiate contact. In the end, they may grow frustrated, disheartened, and might temporarily lose interest and move on altogether.

Incidentally, I conducted several online polls with single gay men to find out if they preferred to ask a guy out or if they preferred the guy to ask them out. 89% preferred to have the guy ask them out. When you expect someone else to ask you out, then you are operating from the feminine receptive energy. If 89% of the prospects are in the feminine energy, then no one gets asked out. 11% get asked out if there is a match to begin with. The majority of those polled remained single and frustrated over having no movement in the love and dating department. They are all waiting for each other to ask the other one out. There's going to be quite a long wait.

The best-case scenario is where the feminine energy person transfers into the masculine energy by biting the bullet and going after the one they have their eye on. The other person is still in the feminine receptive energy and therefore accepts the proposal. Now the connection has been made. Movement continues to happen and grow pending they both vacillate one another's energies accordingly from masculine to feminine.

One woman is the primary breadwinner and makes the bulk of the survival income. She is an executive who runs her own company. Her husband works from home, but doesn't make as much money and takes care of the children. The wife in this scenario is the masculine energy, while her husband is the caring compassionate feminine energy. This doesn't make him any less of a man or her any less of a woman. This relationship works because they have incorporated the right balance of energies.

If a couple is two people of the same gender, then

this law still applies. If you examine the successful long-term unions, you will notice that one of the partners tends to exude the more masculine energy, while the other is the more feminine energy. They might flip flop where it toggles from masculine energy to the feminine energy field. This is depending on what's going on or what needs to get done. Exceptions can always be made to a generalization.

The stereotype is that women are looking for emotional support, while men are looking for sex. A woman might have a difficult time connecting with a man if she hasn't connected with him on an emotional level. A man might have a difficult time connecting with a woman if he hasn't expressed himself through sex.

This concept applies to the masculine/feminine energies. If a man or woman is exuding the feminine energy, then he/she will want to connect on an emotional level first. However, a man or woman is exuding masculine energy if he wants to connect on a mental level first. If he feels the person is a buddy type, then he's more opt to being open to sex with that person.

Same sex couples offer another challenge. Two people of the same gender may seem to be a super easy connection due to both genders understanding what it's like to be that gender, but that's a myth since all people are complicated regardless of their gender or orientation. You could have one male being the more emotional one craving emotional support from his partner, while the other is less talk and more action. That guy is the more masculine energy of the two partners. Two women would be the same concept.

One heterosexual man attempted to debunk the

myth that men do not expose their feelings. He is a heterosexual man who said that some have called him sensitive while others have said passionate. He added that he's the type of guy who will fly his fist into a wall, but on the flip side he can write a poem. His question was, "Am I too sensitive?" Some women/men want a guy who is sensitive and passionate, rather than distant, aloof, and insensitive.

Sensitivity and being passionate can go hand in hand, but they're quite different. Being sensitive can mean that you have an artistic creative side and are in tune to others feelings as well as your own. Passionate is taking that sensitivity to another height. It's sensitivity with some fiery emotions or temperament. It can be someone who is hypersexual and prefers the long sensual kind of lovemaking. It can also be someone who puts their whole selves into whatever they undertake whether it's a career or a relationship. The sensitive more passionate partner is exuding the feminine energy in this state.

If the man in the relationship doesn't feel the support from his partner whether the partner is a woman or a man, then he will shut down and distance himself. He needs to know his partner is fitting the definition of a partner. This mean the potential mate is much like a business partner where both work together as one having a sense of camaraderie. You offer mutual support the way you would with a best friend.

Relationships reach a place of strain when both partners don't understand when to willingly and graciously give the other partner space as required. Many men primarily need constant bouts of space otherwise the connection will suffocate and so will he.

This is why you sometimes hear stories about the guy going out with his buds to have a beer, watch a game, or tinker around with gadgets in the garage. The man in this instance is exuding the masculine energy of strong silence and not needing any kind of emotional distraction, but seeking out an outlet for action. While the woman or feminine energy desires to talk about a situation is exuding the feminine energy. This person ends up calling up a friend to gab. This energy vacillator applies to all connections regardless if it is romantic, friendship, family, or business. And whether or not it's coming from the man or the woman.

The genders of human souls have drastically shifted to be equal across the board, which means it's now more common to see some women also desiring this space and not wanting to talk about anything serious, while the man wants to talk about it. This is the role reversal of energies we've noticed evolving. Women tend to want to bond even closer to their partner when they're having troubles. The differences of the genders involved are especially evident here. The feminine energy wants to talk about it, while the masculine energy wants to take action to fix it and move on. You also have astrological factors and one's upbringing to take into account when studying the complexity of an individual.

With same sex couples there is another rough dynamic depending on what kind of energy the partners exude. I've consulted with same sex couples where there were two males and one of them was the more emotional one demanding constant attention from the other. The more he did that, the more the other guy withdrew and grew more distant and less talkative. Pressuring the non-communicative guy to talk will only shut the communication down. A non-talkative guy doesn't open up to emotional demands regardless of his sexual orientation. You likely wouldn't charge at a friend that way, so you'll want to consider approaching the guy as you would one of your friends.

I've also received cases where it's a male-female dynamic with the female wanting to talk to her guy about something, but the more she does, the more the guy pulls further away. The one pulling away is the masculine energy who requires space. The more you hound that person, the worse it will be. This is because the male/masculine energy prefers to take action to correct something, rather than talk about it. It's the same concept as someone who doesn't care for repetitive work based meetings. They find it to be a waste of time and a bunch of nonsensical hot air blowing around, instead of getting to work and doing the job.

During my past work endeavors, I was never a fan of the meeting. I found them mostly to be mundane and counterproductive in general. I exude the masculine energy in this case where I prefer diving right on in and doing the work immediately. There are exceptions where sitting down to have a meeting about something is necessary, otherwise give me the bullet points quickly and let's move on and not dwell on it. This is more along the lines of daily meetings as opposed to beneficial once in awhile meetings.

There are also male-female dynamic relationships where the female is the one in the masculine role and needing that space, while her man is in the feminine role demanding emotional attention. This doesn't make anyone less of a man or a woman. This has to do with energies and ensuring that it's balanced within the relationship.

Is there also balance with your work and personal life? Missy explained that her boyfriend Tom is distant and cold. Tom has compassion and cares, but he doesn't express it the way Missy would like. There is no reassurance about their connection coming from Tom. Missy heads to work where her colleagues are distant and cold as well too. This isn't in a nasty mean way. Her colleague's personalities happen to be the quiet serious distant types who do their job and leave. There is no balance within the team where another personality in the mix offers warm and cheery sociability.

When Missy leaves and goes on a date with Tom, she finds Tom has the same energy as her colleagues. There is no cheer in Missy's life as she prefers a little enthusiasm and personality at some point in her day. This can cause one to feel glum, even if everything in your life is going well. Missy has a job that pays her bills. She has a boyfriend to go on a date with, but she still feels despondent about it. There isn't enough balance of cheer from either her colleagues or the guy she's dating.

Missy used to work the afternoon shift and her team at the company during that shift was always cheery and sociable brightening up her day. She explained all would be well if either her current morning shift teammates were bright and cheery or if her boyfriend was. This is playing a part in the lack of balance in her life. When you're experiencing unhappiness where the source is not understood, then look at the kind of energies around you and make adjustments where necessary.

CHAPTER ELEVEN

COMMUNICATING COMPROMISE

*Y*ou've met someone you like and this person likes you too. There is no greater starting off point when there is the initial spark between two people on the same page with the same interest. You're hoping it will grow into something resembling a committed relationship eventually. When you plague your mind with thoughts wondering what's going on with you and this new person, then you've begun the practice of sabotaging it. Allow the process of coming together to happen naturally. It won't happen overnight even after you've both discovered it's a match. Enjoy this new connection without suffocating it with unnecessary demands and worry. Worry and concern cripple a relationship connection, even if the effects are not witnessed right away as a result of this anxiety. You're still creating a potential self-fulfilling prophecy. What is to come is then set in motion. It will continue until you shift your thoughts and emotions into *feel good* thoughts and feelings about this lovely new connection that's taken place. Live in the moment and enjoy the connection without fear of where it's headed. Avoid worrying over the direction that you hope the connection will go.

Relationships are exciting when you place zero pressure on them. You're both enjoying yourselves with one another. It's intended to be a celebratory event and a safe haven where you can both blossom and grow together, rather than allowing it to grow hostile and self-destruct due to the actions of the ego part of oneself.

There will be a point during the course of dating someone where you will establish what you are. Will it be casually dating, exclusively dating, or a relationship? This question shouldn't come up or be a concern within the first two to three months. The exceptions are those couples who immediately agree they are an item. It doesn't always happen that quickly, and have no fear if the one you're casually getting to know hasn't reached that point within the first couple of months of knowing what you are. They're currently enjoying the experience of getting to know you. Typically, the shotgun relationships where both people have agreed they are an item after a first date have a far less chance of lasting. When one starts up a relationship abruptly, then it will often end just as unexpectedly. Those who are restless to get into a relationship will be just as impatient to get out of it.

If you're seeing one another sporadically about a couple of times a month, then this is a casual dating connection until you both have the talk about what you are.

You cannot make anyone do anything they don't want to do. You also can't ride people to change to be the way you want them to be. The process of changing is a long one that can only be decided by the individual. Pushing a loved one, a friend, or family member to change into something you can tolerate and be content

99

with will only result in frustration and disappointment. Accept someone as they are or let them go and move on. Avoid going around in circles wondering if someone is going to ever give you what you desire, because that rarely happens. Human souls are individuals and need unrestricted freedom to be themselves. They are not slaves intended to be under someone else's control. If you stifle someone's individuality in any kind of relationship, then you will eventually witness the end of that connection.

One of the far less pleasant scenarios are where you like someone as a friend, but they are intent in forcing you into a stronger close love relationship with them. You're torn because you do enjoy this person and want to be friends with them, but you don't have romantic feelings for them. You might find them attractive, but there isn't enough there for you to merge with them into more than that. I understand this well and have been the one where the other person meets me and is suddenly slamming on the gas afterwards to let me know I'm the one for them. I'm thinking, "How did I get into this? And what am I going to do? I really like this person....as a friend. I think they're attractive, but I don't have romantic close feelings for them on a higher chemistry level. I'm going to end up hurting them when they discover I'm not as interested as they are of me."

This is not a fun space to be in, but you cannot worry if you're going to hurt them or not. The longer you drag it on, the more you will hurt them. You need to be direct and upfront with them as soon as possible and as soon as you know you have no interest. Tell them exactly how you feel. You really like them, but you don't have romantic feelings for them. You might manipulate the truth a bit to spare them from receiving an ego blow by saying, "I'm not looking for a relationship right now with anyone, but I'd like to continue seeing you as a friend." There's nothing wrong with manipulating the truth slightly if you fear hurting someone. What you don't want to do is lead them on if you have zero intention of ever merging in with them beyond a friendship. If you find that while hanging out with them as a friend that they seem to have a deeper interest in you, then you may need to be prepared to distance yourself from them for awhile.

If one person has multi-layered love feelings for you and they constantly hang out with you, then those feelings may expand and grow creating an ever bigger scene if you have friendship feelings for them and nothing more.

Unhelpful advice that anyone could give someone who is having issues in their relationship is to leave the one they are with so they can have the potential of a brighter future connection with someone else. Your friends and family may have a tendency to do that. Their hearts may be in the right place, but when you're having issues in your relationship, then it's wise to go to a specialized counselor in love relationships who is emotionally detached from your situation. Your friends and family are not objective enough to offer sound enough advice that is objective. Neither is asking strangers in a forum or social media arena. They are not a qualified specialist, and don't always have your best intentions at heart. You need an objective party who understands the nature of love, relationships, and the human condition while remaining neutral emotionally.

The higher self-perspective is a little different

when it comes to how soul connections and relationships are currently viewed. The easy answer is that you work it out with the person you're with rather than leaving every single person who doesn't measure up to your standards. The exceptions are abusive relationships. When you're in a relationship that is abusive, such as verbal, emotional, or physical, then it's time to consider dissolving the connection safely.

Communication is a vital beneficial factor for any relationship to thrive. If you do not communicate, then your relationship will die. It's not going to work if only one of the two of you communicates regularly, but the other partner doesn't or is not super responsive. Communication is more than having regular communication going on back and forth whether in person, texting, email, or phone. When you and your partner communicate with one another, are you listening and hearing what the both of you have to say? If you get defensive every time your partner communicates about something bothering them, then your mate will communicate with you less. You'll eventually realize that months have gone by and you're telling a friend, "It seems like we don't communicate anymore."

Problems cannot be swept under the rug. Ignoring something and hoping it will go away doesn't work. When time passes and nothing is said, then unhappy resentment grows. You have to face it head on. Being an efficient problem solver in a relationship also carries over to other areas of your life such as your work life, career, hobbies, and friendships.

Couples that have an open line of communication with their partner tend to have longer lasting relationships. There might be times where you feel your lover is not really listening to you or shuts you down over a touchy topic. You'll need to say in a calm non-confrontational tone something such as, "I'd really like to sit down and talk with you about this as it's still bothering me."

If your partner truly cares about the relationship and you, then they will be concerned that something is troubling you and will want to work it out. A loving partner cares just as much about you and the partnership as they do themselves. This should be reciprocated where you offer that same loyalty in return.

There is a fine line between discussing certain issues calmly to bringing them up in a dramatic way that have more to do with your ego demands. You'll want to keep your ego in check when communicating and avoid emotional manipulation. Emotional manipulation is passive aggressive where one attempts to illicit a particular response out of their partner by inciting words that can induce feelings of guilt out of them. It throws one for a loop because the person comes at you in a kind and sympathetic way, but then you realize you've been manipulated into acting, thinking, or communicating in a manner that makes you feel uncomfortable. There is no room in a healthy long-term relationship for insecurities, confusion, or emotional manipulation. Emotional manipulation is also when your partner makes indirect statements that confuse you or cause guilt. They will succumb to unhealthy communication by making statements to illicit a particular kind of response from you in order to test you. They might say out of nowhere, "I'm not sure how I feel about us."

Healthy communication is when you both discuss

issues calmly and with love. You both feel safe and comfortable working it out together. You include the other person's feelings and thoughts. You communicate clearly and you genuinely listen to one another. You might take a walk and put your arms around one another and lovingly communicate in order to find a resolution where you're both happy.

If you're the kind of person who is shy, fearful of confrontation, or you battle with articulating your feelings verbally to your lover efficiently, then write a letter. Sometimes letter writing helps matters rather than winging it clumsily through speech. Some tend to communicate better through speech than writing, while others might find writing a letter to be the cowardly way out. It is the cowardly way out if someone breaks up with you by letter, text, phone, or email. If you had an in person love relationship, then you'll want to break it off in person. You owe the person you chose to form an alliance with that much.

Some avoid breaking it off in person as they have no idea how the other person on the receiving end is going to react. They don't want to be anywhere near them when that happens. If the person on the receiving end goes ballistic and starts throwing things, or they quietly break down and cry, then either way it'll be uncomfortable unless you're lucky enough to discover that your partner is in agreement with the split as they've lost interest in you too! If you were adult enough to get into a relationship with someone, then you should be mature enough to end it the right way.

The exception to not breaking it off in person might be if you and this other person didn't know one another that well and were dating for a month or two. In person break ups are more appropriate if you had a long history with the person or were together for more than three to six months.

Writing a letter about something you're afraid to bring up about an issue is better than not saying anything at all. In the end, do whatever is more comfortable for you to get your point across while keeping your partners feelings and considerations to heart as well. Be willing and ready to sit down and discuss what you've written with your partner after they've read your letter.

Avoid arguing with your love partner via text. Serious conversations should be in person. If it's not possible logistically at that moment, then a phone call will suffice. Texting serious conversations is inappropriate and nine times out of ten it's taken the wrong way, misconstrued, or misunderstood. If you're afraid of communicating to your partner via phone or in person, then perhaps you're not ready for a love relationship.

Do you complain about every little thing? You dissect actions that others do to the point where you're annoying everyone around you. Those that are guilty of this are typically unaware of it. Being in tune to everything that is around you and observing how you behave is a significant beneficial component needed in your relationships and all of your dealings in life. Complaining is communicating negatively. Those who complain constantly tend to be unaware they are doing so. When you point it out they will justify it with, "I have something to say and I'm going to say it. I don't think it's complaining."

Being on the receiving end of a nagger is an immediate turn off and a boner killer metaphorically speaking. Pick and choose wisely on what's critical to complain about. This coincides with picking your battles. Not every complaint someone has is warranted. Unless it's life threatening, then it's probably not something to make a big deal about. Rule of thumb is work on complaining less.

Men and women can be significantly different from one another. Both genders wrestle with attempting to figure the other one out. I'll receive messages from women asking, "From a guy's perspective, why do you think he...." Speaking for men is that men are easy. Love them, don't nag them, leave them alone. Men will get irritated if you continue to hound them and it becomes a turn off. While both genders require support from a partner, men tend to prefer partners who support their work and endeavors, while many women require emotional support. Those who are not of either stereotype desire support all around.

There will be lulls in any love relationship at some point. You could suddenly find that you have nothing to say to one another and have exhausted all avenues of conversation. This is one of the reasons that relationships take work. The work is effort that you both apply to the union. When you notice a lull, then you find creative ways to ignite the passion in it. Take regular getaways together as well as frequent breaks from the relationship. This isn't the kind of break where you're no longer in the relationship. On the contrary, this is about having your own independent lives and hobbies that you enjoy alone or with friends outside of the relationship. You have your interests, they have their interests, and then every now and then you come together with your mutual interests. This is bringing in healthy balance to your relationship, and also prevents stagnancy or boredom from setting in by being around one another 24/7 indefinitely.

Others have complained that their love relationship seems to have lost its spark. It feels more like roommates living together. I'm not sure what they were expecting when they got into a love relationship. You are living together and splitting the costs on things as if it is a roommate. What differentiates the roommate from the love relationship is you cross the friendship line. You include intimacy into your connection. You take care of your relationship and nurture it, because like a plant your union needs water to thrive and grow. There is going to be tension, disagreements, a lack of sex, and mood swings. What would contribute to the demise of the connection is if those negative traits become a permanent part of your relationship, and neither step up to the plate to mend it. When all you do is quarrel when you see each other, then that's a slow way to kill the relationship. Who wants to be involved in a connection where all you do is bicker.

Relationships grow more distant and fall apart when you do not spend time together and communicate. This is why most long distance relationships do not work and nor do relationships based on living far apart on the map. There are always exceptions to this rule. You might be someone whose significant other is on a war tour abroad. In that particular situation you're a supportive, loving, and loyal partner knowing that they are fighting for their country. They are doing a noble act that will eventually end. Long distance relationships can work if both people have plans to one day live in the same city as the other. They make the long distance connection work through regular communication and trust.

The long distance relationships that have the most strain are the ones where both partner's live hours or more apart. They see each other irregularly with little to no communication. Communicating daily with honesty is essential and can keep it alive pending both partners are mature and adult about it by taking it seriously as if it is their own business.

When the person you're with reaches out to you to talk about something they're doing or want to do, then they're doing that to feel your support and love for them. Sometimes it's to get their mind off something upsetting in another part of their life. Maybe they want to be cheered up, hugged, or even made love to. Other times it's to communicate and talk something out. If someone isn't interested in any of those things, then why are you in a relationship?

You shouldn't have to hide your thoughts and feelings. It needs to get out of you, if even through creative expression. If a person really loves you, then they will want you to be yourself. Most of the time one's close friends are the immediate group where one feels as if they can truly be themselves. With family or a love relationship, there is some measure of not revealing one's inner thoughts or feelings for fear of judgment or retaliation. They don't want to rock the boat.

Communicating is about talking over the little things too. If your mate loves to hold hands and kiss in public, but you don't, then let them know it makes you uncomfortable and that it has nothing to do with them. You just prefer to keep stuff like that private and between you two.

COMPROMISE

Compromising is another essential component in a love relationship's longevity that falls under the form of positive communication. There will be times where the both of you are looking to make a decision, but strongly desire something different and opposing from one another. It would be unusual to be with someone where you always agree on every single shred of decision-making, which can also make for a boring connection in the eyes of some. While others find that kind of a match to be super easy going and ideal. Who wants constant friction and drama?

Compromising is when you are both adult enough to meet in the middle to where you are both happy with the outcome. You find some middle ground and let go of any resistance to hang onto the idea that it is your way or the high way. The purpose of soul mate relationships is to assist you in your soul's growth. This means you're presented with ways of doing things that you normally hadn't entertained. Your soul mate pushes you out of your comfort zone or gets you to think about things you hadn't previously considered.

Practical goals can crumble a union if there is no compromise or acceptance. These would be the bigger stuff such as one of you wants children and the other doesn't. One of you prefers to eventually live in a country ranch setting with little to no people, while the other one wants to live in a busy city slammed with people. Those are some pretty big differences that you will want to know about during the initial dating stages. Granted some people change their minds and views over time. One might have desired children in the beginning, but then eight years into the relationship you discover they no longer want kids. Their life goals changed and children are not part of the equation.

Compromise is essential up to a point, but if you're compromising all that you are at every turn, then you run the risk of losing your identity to this person. It's natural to disagree on certain things, but it's another thing to compromise to the point where all you do is go along with your love mate even though you're secretly against whatever is being decided. Resentment starts to grow and build over time for your partner who likely has no idea this is going on within you. Soon you have this ongoing resentment where you don't even know how that energy started.

Compromise is essential in a successful partnership, but not to the extent where you're giving in on every decision made. If you find that to be the case and it causes you internal unhappiness, then it's time to either re-evaluate the partnership and have a serious discussion with your partner, or learn to contribute your choices to the mix too. It's your relationship just as much as it is your partners. Don't give away your power to another as that falls into people pleasing. It's perfectly common to have to compromise with your mate on a regular basis since no two people are the same, but successful couples have basic similar values and desires as the other. They hear each other out and take turns compromising so that both are happy.

I know of a successful relationship where the guy is shy and prefers to be more of a homebody, but his long-term girlfriend is hugely sociable and loves going out with friends to restaurants, bars, or clubs. This couple makes it work through compromise. It doesn't bother her that he prefers to stay home while she goes out, and he doesn't mind that she goes out while he stays home on occasion. It also gives them both that added alone time space that all couples need to keep from getting sick of one another.

CHAPTER TWELVE

SEX AND SEXUALITY

Sex is a highly weighty element for many men and women in relationships. The trend according to some men seems to be that a woman will refuse to give it up until she's ready, but I've heard cases where it's the reverse with the woman wanting it, but the man is not into it. We also saw that in the hit series *Sex and the City*, which revealed women to be just as sexual as men. Men and women are wired differently to an extent. Men have more testosterone and women have more estrogen. This contributes to behavioral differences in the genders. Some of this is a generalized stereotype that has been perpetuated through modern culture. When men make love, they're in it for the moment, but when it's over, then it's done the end. This is not always the case, but generally speaking it is true more than it is not.

Women tend to bond emotionally to the man during sex and many want to cuddle afterwards, but find that that guy doesn't want to do that. Sometimes it's the reverse where it's the man emotionally attaches himself to the woman, and the woman is detached and uninterested.

Same sex couples will experience a similar dynamic

as an opposite sex couple. This is where one of the guys sees sex as sex and nothing else, while the other guy experiences an emotional bond the way a woman might. He latches onto the other guy who attempts to wiggle out of that. People are complicated and not as cut and dry as modern culture makes them out to be. They've always been complicated, but simply faked it and conformed so as not to be ostracized. As Earthly life moved through the sexual revolution beyond 1970, this put all genders and orientations on the same playing field. When a man experiences more emotion than a woman it's no longer looked upon him as being less of a man. The same can be said about a woman who is less emotional than a man.

If the sex dwindles or is non-existent for the man, then this will bother him regardless if he says it out loud or keeps it to himself. This isn't to say that sex is not a central focus for women, but if the relationship is going well in other areas such as emotional fulfillment and a sense of security, then the lack of sex is not the end of the world even if they secretly desire it. This was the general consensus that women brought to my attention. For a man, especially a younger man, a lack of sex can become problematic in a connection.

From a guy's perspective, they cannot cuddle with just anyone, let alone cuddle with someone after sex. They have to be astronomically interested in the person on a profounder level before moving into cuddling. The guy who jumps up and heads out the door immediately after sex is for the same reason. They were not that interested in the person beyond the physical casual sex. The ones that are into you on a deeper level are able to convey that through cuddling.

There is a myth perpetuated that men fear emotion.

Many men who have higher testosterone tend to be less into emotions and more into action, even though there is some level of emotion with action. It's more of the passionate driven emotional variety. Men do not fear emotion. They're not connected to it the way someone else might be. It's not their driving force. When it hits them recklessly, then it can cause confusion or an uncomfortable feeling.

Women grow quiet when they're bothered by something, but men grow quiet when their mind is on other things rather than being slighted. The male emotion is equally complex. You have to take into account other factors beyond the man. It's American men that tend to not be talkative about their feelings and emotions, because there are men from other countries such as Spain or Italy who are equally open about it as women. This is beyond it being the basic nature of man. What needs to be examined is the culture the man was raised in and how that influenced him. By not encouraging emotion in the young male growing up can be problematic when they're older. Those raising the guy are doing him a disservice by not allowing all facets himself to be expressed in a balanced form.

It is interesting to note how men and women are built and wired differently generally speaking. Women have complained that guy's only care about sex and refuse to cuddle afterwards. I've heard from men who like to cuddle and women who are more like the guy running off once they're done having sex. For the most part, men don't particularly feel comfortable with cuddling after sex. When a man orgasms, this releases any bonding feelings that were once present. They suddenly have a temporary detachment to whoever they are with. This doesn't mean they're not interested, but there are chemicals released after he orgasms that can make it uncomfortable to be touched in any form after sex. This disinterest in cuddling between the sexes was exaggeratedly examined in the film, *When Harry Met Sally*. For the record, I'm a guy who likes to cuddle after sex, but in the past I've been selective about who with. Cuddling in the eyes of some men is seen as a more intimate act than sex.

The desire to cuddle afterwards is viewed on a case-by-case basis. People who tend to be more emotional or passionate in nature tend to enjoy cuddling or touching whether after sex or at any other time. While those who are less passionate or emotional and operating on an intellectual level don't crave the kind of touching and cuddling intimacy that someone else might. Those that love to cuddle might only do so when they're experiencing a vulnerable moment or desire a feeling of safety, security, and bonding that cuddling with another can provide. This goes back to childhood and what was given to the child or what was denied. There are endless factors that come into play as to why some men or women prefer to cuddle after sex while others do not.

Some have sex where there is no kissing involved, but strict animalistic primal sex. Kissing is more of an intimate act with someone you are super into or attracted to. If the latter is not present, then one might not be that interested in the person even though they are having sex with them. Many find kissing more intimate than sex. Someone can have sex with you, but they don't want to kiss you.

Touching is another ingredient to incorporate into your relationship. The physical body and the soul longs to connect to that missing piece within them since they entered into a human life. Human souls require and desire some form of touch or contact. It's true that some couples are not physically affectionate and neither think about it or want it. There are still other ways of exchanging affection.

Sometimes the couple gets a rush by sitting on the couch with their mate sharing fun word banter back and forth. Whatever your means of affection are then incorporate it with your partner. Issues will arise if one person doesn't require touch, but the other one does. One of you longs for physical touch, while the other is longing for mental stimulation. If this endures for any length of time untreated, then it could cause friction or frustration. The worst case scenario is when it pushes the connection to break apart. That is unless both parties acknowledge that they will compromise and meet the other half way to give them what they crave.

Those who don't like being touched are not always born that way. Any discomfort they experience with touch has come about from their upbringing where it might have been denied. The opposite extreme is they were smothered by a parent or guardian. When your soul's vibration is high, it does not shun touch. It enjoys giving love and affection. Touching raises the soul's vibration of both partners and diminishes potential health issues. Others might operate purely on an intellectual or mental level where touch is not desired or required. Astrological aspects can also play a part in that too.

There are basic common sense rules to apply in a relationship, but the truth is that you can do everything right and the other person will still leave you. You could be that perfect mate where you're loyal, honest, emotionally available, and supportive. You're passionate, compassionate, loved them up, kissed them, and made love to them. Name every great quality to put into a relationship and you likely did it. You've taken them out and been the sole person who provides on all levels. You've whisked them away on little getaways. You've entertained them and made them laugh. You've assured them that you're in it for the long haul, and you've put them first next to yourself. You take care of yourself inside and out. You're independent and make your own money. You're easy on the eyes. You have all the basic qualities that anyone looking for a life partner wishes for and yet your relationship partner ultimately sabotages it. They might do this either through chatting around with others inappropriately, developing situations on the side with that person, or they end up leaving you.

Why a partner leaves you can be for various reasons. Some people realize they cannot be in a relationship. They've grown disinterested in the person they're with. When you have a world that operates from the space of a short attention span, then this will carry over to their relationships too.

Having positive qualities to contribute to a healthy long-term loving relationship is an exceptional quality, but it doesn't mean the other person won't suddenly leave you. When that happens, know that it has nothing to do with what you did or didn't do. This is the other person's journey and you cannot force someone to stay with you, or like you the way you want them to no matter how hard you try. When you follow these common sense rules, then the right person for you will stay. Love is blind where you can fall for someone who displays red flags from the beginning, yet you fail to notice it while in the throes of the honeymoon phase of love.

When you fall in love, this releases the hormones dopamine and oxytocin. These are feelings that create an overall sense of positive well-being. You're basically high on life! You're suddenly focused and energetic able to accomplish things that you had previously put aside before you fell in love. This is also why being in love and having a love partner is beneficial to your heart and overall well-being. It's also why those who are in love with you can stop at nothing to get you or be with you. This is because in essence love is like a drug. It gives them that natural high where they'll stop at nothing to obtain. The danger of this is that you may be in love with someone who doesn't share those feelings. There is nothing worse than being in love with someone and they're denying it because they're not interested. You'll notice that it doesn't necessarily detour someone from giving up. They will grow miserable or depressed not being able to be with you. Someone might start lashing out or resort to stalking behavior to get as close to you as possible.

Not all loyal loving relationships are sexual in nature. They cannot be stereotyped like that since all connections are diverse and varying from one another. Some couples have a high sex life where it happens daily if not every day, while others will go for weeks, months, and years without having sex. A long-term loyal love relationship does not automatically mean a high sex life with one another. It may start out as highly sexed, but then the couple gets into the day to day grind of life and find they connect less physically.

People end up in loyal long-term love relationships

for various reasons and not all of them are sexual.

Some couples are not that physical and nor do they express themselves physically in a relationship. There are the obvious reasons why, such as they have physical or psychological sexual challenges. Maybe the guy is impotent or the girl does not get aroused easily. There are also super religious couples that only mate for procreation purposes. Some couples reach a certain age where sex is not something they desire, but they express intimacy in other ways. You've likely witnessed older couples express love with one another by holding one another's hand. There are many forms of connecting physically beyond sex, even though holding hands would fall into the realms of physical pleasure.

CHAPTER THIRTEEN

THE INS AND OUTS OF MARRIAGE

The reasons most marriages and long term relationships fail is due to the human ego. When you use little dark ego in your day-to-day dealings, then the smoother and clearer the ride. Marriages and long term relationships had a greater chance of lasting pre-1970. This is because most did not view relationships as having an out. They knew it was a life sentence they wanted to be in. They had honor, commitment, and applied teamwork to keep it going. Family and security was equally important. They did not allow their ego or selfish desires to take them over causing the kind of irreparable damage that we see today. This doesn't mean that marriages were not without their problems, but people were more inclined to working together to smooth them out. They were realistic and mature knowing there would be issues on occasion.

Men who feel that marriage does not benefit the man are a result of either being burned by a past love interest, or being taught by their peers, society, and popular culture that there is no benefit to men. The man gets married, then the relationship ends and his wife sues him to obtain half his income for the rest of his life. It's reasonable that a man would be hesitant or completely against marriage if that's the case. There are situations where the guy takes the woman to the financial cleaners, although not as prevalent as the reverse. I know of a successful woman who had to pay her ex-husband nearly $30,000 a month in alimony because she made the bulk of the money. In this rare instance, he took her to court for it.

In the current top 25 list of most expensive divorces at the press time of this book, 24 of those people who had to pay out the largest alimony to a spouse were men. There was only one woman in that list of 25 most expensive divorces, and that was the entertainer Madonna who had to pay her second ex-husband roughly $76–$92 million in alimony. You can see what the ratio is between men and women having to do a pay out of alimony in a divorce statistically. This is a big reason why many men avoid marriage regardless of how much they make.

No one wants to see what they built be taken down brick by brick by an ex. This is an alarming situation no matter who is doing it. This is why there are prenuptial agreements offered to couples, even though it might not be the most romantic request to ask a potential mate to sign. You have to protect your assets regardless if you're a man or a woman. Protecting your assets is protecting yourself. Provisions can be added where the one making the bulk of the money agrees to a particular payout in the event of a divorce.

Some automatically believe that if their mate asks them to sign a prenuptial agreement when they get married that they don't believe the marriage will last. When you're in the hazy throes of marriage, love, and romance, then bringing an enforceable prenuptial agreement into the set up can come off like a damper in the rug for some people.

You have to protect yourself and your assets. The mate that is intended for you will not be offended. If they are, then you might look at that as a sign that they want to own you. They will look at it as if you're attempting to keep the two of you separate. Those that have no problem understand the reality. They're not marrying you for your money and assets are they?

In the result of a divorce, people tend to be angrier and into exacting revenge over a mate for allowing the connection to break apart. They will go after their mate and attempt to clean them out. If you have a legal document preventing that from happening ahead of time, then you are protecting yourself. It's no different than insuring your car, your home, or your health. A prenuptial agreement doesn't mean one doesn't trust the marriage will not last.

My father was married once and that was to my mother. Even though he still had long-term love relationships after they split, he informed me that he would never get married again. This was more due to being taken to the cleaners. A long term best female friend of mine whose been married four times said, "You can touch anything, but a man's bank account, otherwise you'll have trouble."

The men who found marriage to be pointless believed that cohabitation was okay. They see cohabitation as having all of the positive benefits that marriage would offer and none of the negative losses that occur should the relationship end. While the other men felt that men who do get married is mostly out of pressure from their mate, family, or their surrounding culture demands it. Pressuring anyone into getting married is against the Universal Law since you are interfering with that soul's free will choice. The United States has grown less demanding of expecting people to get married. It's no longer seen as the thing that everyone needs to do. Americans are lucky if they find someone to date as it is, let alone marry since statistically speaking finding a love partner has become more challenging than marriage.

Every individual has their own view that is not always in alignment with one another. One cannot fully speak for an entire race, religion, gender, political affiliation, or sexual orientation. This is when you fall into stereotypes, which are not based in truth. It is the not thought out point of view infiltrating one's personal experiences for having been in loveless marriages with gold diggers.

Women have felt messed with in marriages through a partners abuse or philandering, and subsequently taken their guy to court for monetary gain after their marriage has come to an end. It's their way of striking back. Some men stay in loveless relationships in order to avoid having to divorce and pay half their income to their mate. There are also cases where it was the man that took the woman to court since she was the financially successful one in the duo. This is all about money, which is the darkness of ego.

Times have changed over the centuries and more people than not have moved into the practice of cohabitation in a relationship rather than full on marriage. They feel the commitment to one another is enough and do not require that 'piece of paper' legally binding them. Part of this has to do with attitudes of the modern day era. There is less pressure to get married. It is no longer mandatory or expected by society.

There are many positive legal benefits to marriage especially for those couples that stay together into old age and the departing of their lives. If your partner ends up in the hospital, it is easier to visit them if you're married to them, than it is as a registered domestic partner. If you've been in a lifelong relationship with someone and yet there is no legal document stating so, then you can run into financial challenges down the line should your partner pass away or ends up in the hospital. There are more protective laws if you're legally married. This is one of the reasons that marriage is beneficial to many couples that are concerned with their future security.

Times are especially tough where ones future is concerned that it is ironic that more people are not joining up in long term relationships. Unless you're a Doctor or a Lawyer making enough income to last until your death, then it helps to have that love partner in crime with you splitting the costs.

The world doesn't value long term relationships the way they once did. This progressive ideology is cute when you're twenty-five, but as you get older and become less obtainable it becomes more challenging. Many will wish they had this love partner in crime when they realize everyone has disbursed and their health is gradually failing.

If your partner dies and there is no Will or Trust, then the state will dictate what happens to their assets, but if you're married then it'll go to you before anyone else, including a blood relative. If your partner dies, you'll receive their social security benefits. The same applies for pension plans, IRA's, etc. You don't think about those things when you're 30 as you do when you're 60 and over. This is also what many against marriage neglect to take into account when they're thinking about their future. People get married to have that partner in crime, a friend, and companion as well as to be secure in older age. Many of those things dissolve away as you grow older. Friendships diminish or they move away or pass on.

Marriage or being in a long term love relationship enables two people who love one another to join in things together that would be more challenging if they were single. It's easier to live in a bigger place when you are with someone contributing half of the rent or mortgage. It's easier to purchase a home having that co-signing love partner who contributes to it as well.

*?*ve had countless dysfunctional relationships with people who were unable to sustain the long haul, but that never stopped me from believing that when I'm with the right one it'll work out fine. When you're compatible with someone else, then neither of you have to try as hard as you would with someone you don't get along with much. Since many will get involved with someone they're physically attracted to first, there is little time spent seeing if you have what it takes to go the distance.

This world is driven by selfish narcissism. It has trained others to be incapable of sustaining a long-term relationship. The heavy rule of the darkness of ego sells narcissism and self-interest to the masses all over the media and social media.

You cannot be happy with someone else if you're not happy with yourself, or if your life isn't where you want it to be. No one truly completes you and if that's what you're looking for you'll be gravely disappointed. Complete yourself and then open the door to allow another in with you to join in the fun.

There are many couples that find one another and live happily ever after. One couple has been married for decades. They both separately said to me, "And it just gets better and better." They evolve together and are doing it because they love each other and want to share their life as a team. They do not feel pressure, but comfortable with one another.

Loving someone is not the same as liking them. You like someone, but you don't marry them. You marry the one you love. This isn't misplaced puppy dog love, but the kind of love where you have their back. You support them when needed. Love is stronger than liking someone when it's real love. Liking someone is settling for them because there is nothing else. You have some measure of emotional detachment to the point where revealing any level of passion is against your nature. Love is unconditional and comes without demands. There is no fixed formula or answer to reach that state of unconditional love since all couples are different. People are complex beings and when you mix one multifaceted being with another, you're going to double the complexity.

The key components to making it a success is to love and support your partner. They should be thought of as your right hand teammate. You are compassionate with each other. You listen to one another while also communicating your feelings honestly and openly. You both have the mindset that you intend to be together until the end. You are forging an alliance and a company with them. When your business is in trouble, you find ways to save it or improve it. This is what you do when you're in a love relationship.

If there are issues, then you discuss it calmly with your partner as to what you can both do to improve it. If one of you is feeling neglected, then you talk to your partner. They are supposed to be your companion and one of your best friends. Whenever someone has a problem in their relationship, they immediately race to their friends. Perhaps you are more comfortable going to them instead of your partner about a serious issue. You don't go to your partner as you don't want to rock the boat and prefer to avoid potential confrontation. You're afraid your partner might get defensive or they will leave you. If your partner is going to do the latter, then they're not worth being in a relationship with. Your partner is supposed to be safe haven and someone you feel you can trust and open up with, otherwise why are you with them?

There is no fixed formula for making a true unconditional relationship work since it's a mutually agreed upon and understood formula made by both parties. Unconditional relationships are also not 100% accurate, because unconditional means *without condition*, and you have conditions when in a relationship. You have conditions that your partner doesn't cheat on you. Right there you now love with conditions. But you can get as close as possible to unconditional love while easing up on issues. Unconditional love is a difficult trait to reach. Everyone places conditions on love to one extent or another. You want someone who is loyal, in it for the long haul, and sticks around. As soon as you have the lists, then you love with conditions. If you can get pretty close to unconditional, then that is miraculous.

Be affectionate with your partner by saying what you mean and meaning what you say by demonstrating that through action. Words are empty and meaningless unless you back it up with action. Hold hands, kiss, bond, and talk regularly. This includes spending at least once a day connecting if only for fifteen minutes. That's not an outlandish demand to put in a little bit of effort into one another. Appreciate your partner and show gratitude. This includes being enthusiastic when either of you accomplishes something in either of your lives. Ask questions about it, show enthusiasm, and be supportive.

Too often couples that become comfortable with one another start to get sloppy where they are taking each other for granted. This isn't always done on purpose. You've reached the space where you're comfortable in the connection that you stop thanking them for things they do. You stop saying kind loving words to one another. When your mate is down and depressed, then find ways to cheer them up and get them out of the house. Motivate and encourage the one you're with to progress, grow, and build themselves with you. As always it should be reciprocated in order to make for a healthy balanced relationship.

Long-term love relationships have an endless list of positive health benefits. Part of this is because when the two people in the relationship show mutual respect and support, then this helps push one another to greater heights in their life. The positive energy of support excites someone to keep going.

There will be challenges in any relationship, including the loving positive ones. The difference is in how the couple handles conflict between one another. An unhealthy couple will attack or criticize the other person's personality, looks, or behavior, while a healthy couple will never resort to such low energy bullying. They will be lighthearted, show affection, and understanding that they recognize their partner is upset. They are willing to meet half way on the matter.

From a spiritual perspective, there is no need for marriage. When you're on the Other Side, it's an eternity. There is no ending of the soul's life. Imagine being married to the same person for thousands of years that never ceases. While on the Earth plane, human life came up with marriage until death do you part. Spending a human life with someone is much shorter than an eternity.

CHAPTER FOURTEEN

MONOGAMY VS. ADULTERY:
IN THE BOXING RING

*T*here are no two relationships that are alike. Every couple agrees on how they'd like to define the relationship to be for them. They may mutually decide that it is a monogamous relationship, while other couples might choose to have the agreement that it is okay to have sex with other people outside of the relationship. Some call this an *open relationship*, when that is more of a fancier title created over the years that ultimately means *friends with benefits*.

It does not matter how you choose to define or title your relationship as long as both people in the connection are cheerfully in agreement of the arrangement. At that point, who is to decide what the relationship should or should not be.

Labels and titles are words human beings give others to describe something or someone at that particular period in history, but they don't have any substance in spiritual truth. If you look back on Earth's history, you'll notice some words that were used to define one thing were changed over the centuries to match the fads of that time. For example, the word *awful* today is used to describe something that is distasteful to you, but there was a time when awful meant something else entirely. It was intended to mean being in awe or splendor. *Naughty* used to mean you have nothing, then it was used to describe being bad or evil. In today's modern day age it means behaving badly or being indecent. The word *troth* was used to describe being loyal to someone or pledging your faithfulness or honor. Now we just say we're loyal rather than troth.

Being loyal in a connection is beyond not cheating. Those interested in long term love relationships expect the person they're with to be loyal. It's automatically assumed to be a given. It's understood that you don't stray or cheat on your partner, otherwise it's viewed as a betrayal. You're lacking in integrity at that point. Some take it another step further and view chatting inappropriately with others to be a cheat. It may not carry as meaningful of a weight if the partner had sex with someone outside of the relationship, but it is still seen as a form of betrayal. Chatting inappropriately with others can eventually turn into more in many cases, but if that's the kind of person you're in a relationship with, then it's better to find that out sooner than later.

One would think it would be common sense to not cheat if you're committed to someone, but adultery has been a lifelong problem for many in relationships. You're with someone who cannot control their impulses.

Being loyal in the grander sense means being supportive and backing the person you're with in whatever endeavors they choose to do. Maybe you might not approve of what your partner wants to do, but when you respect them and the choices they make, then you are supporting them.

There will be challenging times and awesome times even in the most perfect love relationship. You both stick around and stand by one another regardless. It's not considered cool to walk away from relationships over the tiniest shred. Loyalty is a basic value incorporated into strong partnerships and families. Mafia members are known to valuing loyalty to the extreme, therefore your relationships should be able to pass the mafia test. Have faith and devotion in each other even when there is a lull. People work as a team in many of their jobs, but many struggle with applying that same dedication to their interpersonal love connections.

There has always been great debate about the nature of the open relationship. Those I interviewed tended to scoff at the phrase indicating it's not something that is taken seriously. While the remainder added, "As long as it's not hurting anyone, but it's not for me." Overall I discovered more people than not were against the open relationship platform. It is more of a personal preference fetish and fad that started during the sexual revolution around the 1970's and beyond. This is when the shift happened on the planet where moral views were less accepting. This kicked off during the hippie movement of free love. Hippies weren't necessarily anti-marriage, but more about not wanting the law to dictate how all relationships should be, which is fair enough. As previously stated, as long as both people in the connection are in agreement, then that is all that matters.

An open relationship is typically where two people get into a relationship with each other, but they're also allowed to date and have sex with other people without their partner present. Serious relationship seekers ridicule the open relationship methodology. The immediate response was, "Why be in a relationship at all then?" Unfortunately, the responses I received were unable to give a strong enough argument as to why they believe it's the way to go. It might be the way to go for them, but it's not what the majority of human souls look for when interested in getting into a love relationship.

The open relationship practice can work for someone who suffocates easily in a long-term romantic partnership where they feel as if they're in prison and there is no way out. They can't bear the thought of spending a lifetime with the same person. They would prefer or require a variety of partners. This still doesn't explain the reasons for getting into an open relationship to begin with. The other reason is to split costs. The cost of living and survival is challenging now, especially for one person to be the sole provider on their own. The exceptions are if you're a Doctor, Lawyer, or any other job that pays excessively well.

It doesn't matter what the title of the connection is as long as both people in the connection are on the same page and in agreement of the nature of their relationship. At that point, who is it truly hurting?

There are other relationships where the couple enjoys inviting in a third party or more for sex. One of the main agreements or rules is that the couples will state, "We only play together." This means the couple will not have sex with someone else outside the relationship without their partner present and involved. That set up falls more into the swinger's category.

The most obvious assumption is that when you

get involved in a love relationship with someone that most people assume that you are in a committed monogamous relationship together, and not an open relationship. Why would you bother getting into a relationship if you are not interested in being monogamous and committed to that person? Those in that kind of circumstance may say it's to have a partner in crime to go home to in the end. No one wants to live their lives solo or grow old alone. Yet, those responses were non-existent from the other side and no practical answer was given. In the end, more people have a greater percentage of being a bitter love party of one than ever before in human history. There is no sugar coating the truth that exists among connections today.

It's cute to be anti-relationship when you're in your twenties, but as you grow older and start to notice the signs of aging and that your body is slowly dying, the reality hits you about the physical life. It can scare someone in terms of their future. Will you be old and alone with no one when you are in your senior years? Some are loners at heart and prefer the no people lifestyle, but what happens when you've fallen and no one knows that you can't get up?

As you grow older, you become more set in your ways. This rigidness is not always inviting to a new partner. You're used to being alone that when you end up in a relationship, you're unable to meet the other person half way, and basically don't want to. This points to one who is ruled by their own ego. The ego is selfish and only cares about itself.

I asked a close friend who has always been anti-relationship why he has never craved a love relationship. He said, "I'm not worried. I have you and all of my buddies. We'll all live on the same street as one another."

I said, "You have a point, but how realistic is that many decades from now?"

When you're young there is the fantasy that all of your friends and family will live on the same street. You'll have barbecues and hang out together every weekend. When in reality people change over the years and some drift away or move apart.

One person expressed worry over the idea of ending up in a relationship, but then falling for someone else outside the connection. It got me to thinking that what if that had happened while I was with any of my past lovers. Granted, it never did as it's against my values, nature, and personality, but what if it happened beyond my control? What if for the first time in my relationship history I find that I'm falling for someone else while in my relationship? My relationship history has shown that I have been devoted to the person I'm with at full force. I have too much respect for our connection to go to that other place. Still you can't help but wonder, what if in that rare occurrence this happens.

While single, I've had a history of being out of control sexually until the next soul mate enters the picture, then I stop and remain loyal indefinitely. It's happened for me with every single person I was in a long-term relationship with. It has nothing to do with, "This is how you're expected to be in a relationship."

When I've been into someone and they're into me, then we're mutually into one another. There isn't any room to invite in other people. We have too much respect and interest in one another to entertain that thought. It's not on our radar as we like and love one another.

People have been monogamous for centuries. Human kind progresses technologically by inventing computers, the Internet, telephones, popular culture, the media, and phone apps where you have a candy store of choices, then suddenly monogamy is considered unnatural. The fact that most still disagree with that statement and that committed souls in a loving connection have stood the test of time says otherwise. There are many mammals in the animal kingdom that are territorial and monogamous by nature.

Popular culture has taught one another to cheat and stray. You have to take a look at what became popular during which time period in history to notice that fad beliefs are praised because it's considered trendy at that time amongst popular culture. The culture is ever shifting and changing, so what's popular at one point in history is not during another time period. What's happening today won't necessarily be the norm centuries from now.

To believe that monogamy is unnatural is justifying it as an excuse to cheat. It's coming from a place of selfishness, "I have desires and no one is going to stop me from having desires and acting on them. It's human nature. No one is monogamous."

Desires are harmless pending it's not hurting anyone else, including yourself. Operate through life with integrity and honesty. When you exude those traits, then you are clear from the beginning with someone that you do not believe in monogamy. You are not interested in ever settling down with anyone.

Desire becomes deceit when you've entered a relationship with false pretenses. You are knee deep in the connection and entertaining thoughts of dating or having sex with other people in secret, and then you act out on it. Deceit comes from the beast within. The beast within is the darkness of ego. It says it's okay to do what you please. If you want to sleep with hundreds of people go ahead. The beast tricks your soul by convincing you to act out impulsively. Impulse is a reaction born out of fear and desire that you better get what you want or else. You obtain it, discard it, and then impulsively act on something else. Meanwhile, years have passed and you look back only to discover that you've been going around in circles accomplishing nothing.

Infidelity can be seen as a character flaw where the ego is giving that person permission to cheat. It is giving you clearance to justify why it's okay to cheat. When you make the pact to put your faith and trust in another soul, you assume that it's reciprocated. You are making a commitment and a promise to join in with that person. If you're unable to remain faithful, then don't get involved in a committed love relationship. Look for a friends with benefits situation, pending the other person agrees that this is all they want too.

There are numerous single people all around the world desiring a committed love relationship. They endure the hardships of being single and making decisions alone without a love partner, therefore the non-monogamous person can too. This isn't in judgment on those who do not believe in monogamy, but it's also unlikely that a non-monogamous person would be interested in a love relationship book to begin with. This is about having integrity. You decide what you desire. If you're in a committed relationship, then honor that to build character and soul enhancing qualities. If you're against monogamy, then don't join into a relationship, or get into a connection with someone who doesn't share those particular values. To say monogamy is unnatural is false. It is a value that the person came to the conclusion of because they're too uncomfortable with the thought of being in a long term relationship with one person their entire life. It is assuming it is unnatural due to the influences surrounding the person that is anti-monogamy. It's human nature and natural to be territorial including in interpersonal relationships.

When someone is in a relationship and their partner cheats, then it is seen by them and those around as deceptive. Adultery causes insurmountable pain on another person in the process through being dishonest. This also builds unnecessary Karma.

Those that insist that human beings aren't meant to be faithful are usually the ones secretly desiring to cheat and don't want that kind of judgment should that happen. They want the freedom to sleep with whoever they choose without interference. Therefore, they will justify that people are not meant to be monogamous, so it's understandable that human nature is unable to control itself since we're not any different than an animal, except most animals are monogamous.

You see the beauty in someone's physical appearance, and your senses cannot help notice how someone's physical beauty is awakening parts of you. It's another thing to desire to have sex with that person while you're involved with someone else.

The darkness of ego has caused an immense amount of destruction on human kind from terrorism, to bullying, to hate filled comments. Media, technology, social media, and other similar vices have caused human souls to be disconnected from anything outside of themselves. They've trained one another to desire instant satisfaction. When it doesn't happen immediately, they grow bored and move onto something else. The way others communicate today has trained modern society to be aloof, distant, selfish, and uncaring. The ego is self-absorbed and only wants what it wants and no one else can enter that equation. The ego doesn't take into account someone's well-being. When you take into account the feelings and thoughts of those around you is operating with compassion. Unfortunately, as many will notice, this is not the case unless there is a tragedy.

When someone discovers that a man cheated on his wife the immediate response is, "All men cheat." Or "Human beings are not intended to be monogamous."

You know who said that? An adulterer.

The obsession with not being monogamous has caused others to be distrustful in relationships because they wonder what their partner is doing when they're not with them. This is a painful unhealthy way to live. The higher self's space in one's soul thrives for stability, loyalty, companionship, and security with someone else in a love connection. Even if you don't believe in any of it, you're still having a spiritual experience when you are in a healthy loving relationship.

In a relationship, having concerns wondering if the person you're with is being faithful or unfaithful is not uncommon. This can stem from childhood where perhaps your caregivers were emotionally or physically abusive towards you causing an immense amount of distrust in others upon first meeting. Or you were in a relationship where your partner cheated. You grow to become transfixed on the idea that your new partner is going to cheat at some point too. You worry that another might tempt you outside of your relationship. Or you have secret concerns that you will suddenly fall out of love with your partner and into love with someone else. Those are concerns one shouldn't entertain unless there is valid proof that someone is being unfaithful. Otherwise it will contaminate the energy in the relationship and could eventually cause it to come to an end.

Successful relationship couples that have endured decades together have fallen in and out of love with one another over the course of both their lives. Relationships are filled with peaks and valleys, changes, stagnancy, and movement. This is the way it is with all relationships whether it's friendships, family members, or colleagues. It's especially intense when love feelings are involved.

Human souls are too territorial to not crave monogamy. Watch a Discovery or History channel piece on animals and sex to see how they mate. They are territorial and become angry when another animal is moving in on their mate. It's not allowed in the animal kingdom. Since human beings behave much like the animal kingdom, they are equally territorial. Look at how many crimes of passion have been committed. Or how many men shoved or punched someone else for moving in on their mate. Or how many women tried to run over their man with their car after finding out he's been with another woman. A small percentage believe monogamy doesn't exist, but it's not the general consensus. The ego came up with that way of thinking due to modern day society's influences, but that doesn't mean it's true. It is true for the non-monogamist, but it doesn't mean that all human beings are built that way.

Spirit in Heaven doesn't condone adultery, nor does it mean you'll be punished for all eternity either. At the same time, human souls have free will choice to choose how they want to live while here, pending it doesn't hurt anybody or themselves. They always say that Jesus never said anything about homosexual relationships, but he did say quite a bit about adultery. This is because he doesn't care about the genders involved in a beautiful loving relationship, pending they are faithful. It's being committed and devoted to someone in a loving union that makes him smile.

Love can come close to perfection when all of its imperfections are loved and accepted. Be honest with yourself and with others surrounding your intentions. Follow the wisdom of being authentic and real.

Many are in the throes of facing the reality that they are with someone who is or has been unfaithful, or has been stringing them along. There is little to no honesty in the connections they are in. I have been listening and watching all of the heartache others experience around the world, as well as the struggles that people have today surrounding love. It's an ongoing epidemic for others attempting to connect with anyone in a committed union.

The current age is a selfish world and many in the dating arena operate from that space of courting others for the sole purpose of being a booty call, yet not all are direct about that. It's been increasingly prevalent since the rise of social media and phone apps. They are against being in relationships in general. This is that person's choice to not desire an exclusive love relationship, but be honest with the one you're pursuing. There are too many cases where someone is going after another they have their eye on, leading them on, building a connection with them, only to later reveal, "I don't do relationships."

Popular media is one of the biggest contributors of the anti-relationship movement. They have had an overall negative influence on others being carefree and nonchalant about certain issues such as monogamy. This particular topic has caused irreversible pain, conflict, and heartache in so many people. That's not something to scoff or be blasé about. It's not surprising to know that a great deal of popular media is run by the darkness of one's ego. This is what poorly influences the newer generations and those in the human developmental stages cutting them off from what's outside of themselves through distraction.

Deep down at the soul's core, the soul desires love, companionship, and commitment. The poor influences over the course of one's life confuse that craving with wanting more selfish self-gratifying longings. It has been taught that there is always an easy way out.

I've witnessed connections permanently fall apart unable to regain lift off because one of the partners has access to a phone buddy sex app with a plethora of choices that keep that person consumed and busy indefinitely instead of strengthening their current connections. Others write me after discovering their mate is on a sex or dating app. This causes confusion within them wondering how interested or disinterested their mate is with them. When some confront their mate, the response they get is they are on there for friendships. Those are the connections I've watched eventually end.

When you make the deal to put your faith and trust in another soul, you assume that it's reciprocated. In that act alone, you are exuding integrity. You are making a commitment and an agreement to join in with that person. If you're unable to remain faithful, then don't get involved in a committed relationship. Instead have a friends with benefits situation with someone who desires that too.

I've been courted and pursued in the past not only during research, but in general by those who are married or in a committed long term love relationship. They've approached me to *experiment* so to speak and have explained they have not done this before. This proposal has been made to me by both men and women, gay and straight. And their spouse mate is unaware.

*M*arcus says that Jennifer tells him monogamy is not natural and this confuses him. Why does she tell him that she misses and loves him then? Because someone who is unfaithful or who doesn't believe in monogamy can still feel love for someone else even though they're unable to control their sexual desires and need an outlet to freely express that with more than one person. In this case, she's being honest with him about her feelings about monogamy. She will never be able to be faithful to solely Marcus and at least she's upfront about it.

Someone who does not believe in monogamy shouldn't automatically be called unfaithful. In that particular scenario, Jennifer had been unfaithful and cheated behind Marcus' back. Once that was out in the open, she began to announce that she no longer believes in monogamy. Unfaithful is when you are in a committed love relationship, but you are discreetly cheating on your partner behind their back. Whereas someone can be against monogamy, but have integrity by being direct about that right away with someone that is clearly into them.

Loyalty is lacking in many partnerships today, which is why there are more singles than there are committed connections. There is too much ego being used in human souls that there is no room to invite someone else and their stuff into your life. People are too selfish to be in long-term connections. Relationships require compromise and compassion while allowing the one you're with freedom. Freedom should not be confused with infidelity. Too many demands are insisted upon while in a relationship. Relationships need space to breathe. The second you place co-dependent demands on your partner, you can prepare to kiss the partnership goodbye. It will ultimately end if that continues.

Human souls crave respectful companionship. Now there is a warped movement of being a free for all and having no connection to others whatsoever. If that's the case, then why are you here? What is the point of your existence? Is it to run out and have one sexual experience after another? I can say that because I've done that and been there with so many that I lost count. It's by far not the same as being connected with one person in a profound way. One excuse after another is made to justify cheating or leaving someone.

Monogamy sounds like a dry clinical word, but when you're in this kind of a match, you don't have to address it, since both parties understand it. Neither of you are interested in anyone else. It just never occurs to them no matter how much they're tempted. To be tempted is to operate from ego. People have been with one person for life since the beginning of time. Monogamy will always end up ruling in the centuries to come.

When two people merge into a healthy committed loving relationship, both of the lights in their souls expand, and their vibrations rise. You know the meaning of the word God while in a healthy committed love relationship. Love and joy is what lifts you into that space. There is no limit to what both people are able to accomplish individually while in that match.

CHAPTER FIFTEEN

AFFAIRS AND FLINGS

*A*ffairs and flings in the workplace have been happening in grand abundance for eons. You have two people working together side by side and day after day. They subsequently begin to grow close and develop feelings for one another. You have free will choice to act or not act how you choose. Your soul previously laid out how key circumstances that will come to light while on your Earthly journey. No one tests you in these situations, but yourself.

If you are in a committed relationship and you find that you're falling for your colleague, then that is your choice to decide to go along with it instead of extricating yourself from the temptation. You're attracted and intoxicated by your colleague who you see more than your partner.

Those who work full time at a company or business that is not a solo self-employed home business will spend more time at work than they do at home. If they work in an office or environment with colleagues, then you will see those people more than your own partner. It wouldn't be surprising to find that some relationships begin to form by being in close quarters with the same person five days a week. It is rare that an office romance will turn into a long-term love relationship that lasts until the end of your Earthly life, but there are some exceptions. The question should be is it worth it? Is it worth losing a solid relationship due to developing feelings for someone in the workplace? Not to mention the repercussions pertaining to one's employment. Most places of businesses do not condone office affairs. When the affair ends, then it can cause friction and lawsuits. Both parties can lose their jobs if they're unable to work out the breakup or if it becomes a conflict of interest at work.

It would be easier said that it would not be wise to continue forward with an office affair, but when anyone develops love feelings for another no matter who it is, then there is no stopping them. You cannot help yourself in that instant and only know what you desire.

All of life circumstances that seemingly cause turmoil or uncomfortable feelings are challenges one imposes on themselves through free will actions and choices. It is true that some people have met their soul mate or twin flame while in the workplace. The connection builds gradually over time and they end up spending years or the rest of their lives together. Many well-known actors in the entertainment industry have formed romantic relationships with their cast member colleagues while at work on set. They spend twelve hours plus a day working together for months and a friendship begins to develop. The friendship grows into a deeper bond, closeness, and soon they become a romantic item. There are also the other cases on set where one is a well-known actor who develops a close romantic relationship with a crew member who is unknown to the public.

My father spent the last eighteen years of his life romantically involved with a woman he met in a professional work environment. This woman was fifteen years younger than him and on her second marriage. She left that second marriage to be with my father and they remained together for 18 years and had a child. The only reason they didn't last longer than the eighteen years was because my father passed away. Evaluating how soul mates come together is a case-by-case basis that would need to be examined. Some workplace romances do in fact go the distance, but they are those rare gems where the two people were indeed intended to come together.

Is it cheating if you're not hurting anyone?

Cheating is being intimate on any level with another person other than the person you're supposed to be the most intimate with. This is why cheating is considered by others to be dishonest, unfaithful, and a betrayal. If it's consented by your partner to go have affairs outside your connection, then you have an uncommitted relationship, but you're no longer being deceptive.

Marriage doesn't work for the selfish because you have to take into account your partner's feelings. If you're selfish, then you don't care what they'll think or feel. What you desire trumps how they might take it.

Should you get a divorce or break up from a committed relationship?

If you're in a connection that is abusive on any level, then the short answer is to get out of the connection as safely and quickly as possible. No one should put up with abuse of any kind, on any level, and in any kind of relationship.

If the relationship is not abusive, and you've spent months or years trying to make your relationship work, and yet you're perpetually miserable, or there is no compromise or happy medium, then consider dissolving the connection. Examine the relationship sincerely enough to the point where you are evaluating yourself as well.

Every soul on the planet should be conducting deep non-obscured self-evaluation. Self-evaluation assists you in seeing where you play a part in the result of an action. It helps you grow, change, and evolve. It assists in getting you to make necessary life changes. Looking at what someone else is not doing for you is operating from your ego and putting you into the position of a victim. It's no one's job to fulfill your needs and desires, but your own.

Examine your strengths and flaws with a fine toothcomb. Would you want to be involved with you? Are there traits you have or do that someone might not warm up to? If you're someone who places constant demands in a relationship, then someone like that is typically unaware that they're being like that. They operate with the mindset that they want something and this other person better fulfill it or else. This would then fall into the category of abuse. If your partner is the one that is like that, then that falls into abuse. Abuse of any kind should never be tolerated.

There are relationships where one person throws in the towel at the slightest sign of unhappiness inside. They feel trapped in long-term relationships, but naively get into them anyway.

Natural pessimists get into love relationships on a regular basis and incorporate that pessimism into what could've been a healthy love connection. There are also cases where the person bounces from one relationship to the next. They meet someone new and immediately see it through rose-colored glasses. They're attracted to the newness of this person who is catching their eye. They do everything in their power to get them. After they've obtained the object of their desire, they are wiggling to get out. It's within three to six months in when they start to feel uncomfortable, miserable, and bored in the connection, so they leave the person. Time passes on and they're repeating this pattern with someone new. It's the exact same cycle and pattern with every single person.

The excitement and lust attraction rises with this new potential where you're spending nearly every week texting them daily. You are always together it seems, then within three to six months at some point in there you walk away and repeat. I've watched them recycle this pattern over and over again through the years. This is more the definition of a love addict who is addicted to the love rush high, but once that high begins to dissolve and loses its luster, they are unable to conjure up ways to continue to breath passion into the connection, and like a drug addict they seek out another fix.

It would never be advised to leave a current partnership because it's not up to your standards. Leaving a connection in search of something better rarely comes to be. The grass is not always greener and you wind up in another similar connection that begins to bore you after a certain amount of time. In more cases than not, the connection may be worse or less fulfilling than the previous one. Meet your partner halfway and accept that you won't be able to change some of their annoying habits, and nor will they be able to with you. It'll be like that with whoever you're with, so make your relationship work.

CHAPTER SIXTEEN

AGEISM

*T*he nitty-gritty reality is that every person on the planet is ageing by the minute and there is no way around that. No one will remain youthful looking forever. The quicker you accept and make your peace with that in an ageist world, then the smoother the ride will be. Appreciate who you are and how you look regardless of your age. Love yourself inside and out by also accepting what you perceive to be a flaw whether physical or internal. You are loving and magnificent more than you can comprehend. Everything is temporary including the body you inhabit. Make the most of it and avoid harshly criticizing yourself. There is someone for everyone on this planet.

Ageism is discriminating against anyone because of how old they are. One could say that young people face some measure of discrimination such as being too young to partake in something, but that doesn't carry the same weight. It's also temporary and not nearly as discriminatory as older ageism. Age discrimination is targeted to those who are of older age in Earth years.

It's met with criticism, disdain, attacks, and bullying.

Age discrimination rose during the technological period when popular culture began force-feeding the masses images of hard-bodied young people as desirable and anyone else outside of that as not. Now everyone is obsessing over their appearance to an unhealthy degree. This put it into people's minds to view aging as a negative flaw, but that mindset is someone living in Fantasyland. The reality is everyone is aging every second and will continue to until their body gives out and is no longer whole.

Generally, someone considered old or discriminated against is typically aged thirty-five and above, but ageism can be noticed as early as thirty years old. There was a time when it was classy to respect your elders. Many older people are stronger, wiser, and experienced having been through a great deal more.

There are quite a number of classy people of all ages who respect anyone of any age. The ones who are younger with that mindset will go far due to having that broader view. Not everyone who is of older age is necessarily stronger or wiser. Someone can be evolved at thirty-five, but another person who is seventy-five resides in a space of continuing to view circumstances in a limited way.

The younger demographic has a greater shot at obtaining a lover than someone who is older. The older you get, then the more set in your ways you are, which rules out more potentials. Your standards are also higher where you're looking for a quality mate. A younger person may have a greater shot, but not necessarily in obtaining someone of substance. They usually base their attraction to another purely on someone's looks. It's that hot looking guy or hot girl they got to have. They find out the hard way or through experience that this doesn't equate to any other kind of compatibility. A younger person may have a greater shot at attracting in someone, but not necessarily in obtaining someone of substance or keeping them there.

You can see through flaws and potential challenges with someone quicker at aged fifty than you can at age twenty. If you're forty-five and looking for a committed partner for life, it's highly unlikely you'll go for a twenty-three-year-old who rides a skateboard and is without a job. Who knows, maybe you will. Love is unexpected and unpredictable with the least likely of people you would have typically not chosen.

The more quality you expect from a partner, the more this diminishes the potential soul mates you'll be attracted to or even pay attention to for that matter.

Popular culture has amplified age discrimination and trained others to see anyone over a certain age as undesirable. Those open to people from all walks of life will beg to differ. The truth is that this is a mixture of both fact and myth. Those with ageism issues are not someone anyone would want to get involved with anyway, since that is someone who thinks and operates in a limited way. This limited perception is carried over to other areas of their life. They have issues that extend beyond ageism and typically don't accomplish much as it is. How can you when you view life through a false filter? If you're twenty-six with age issues, it won't be long before you turn your head and you're thirty-five struggling to find a mate because you're no longer seen as desirable.

I've conducted social experiments that included me removing my age from app profiles. Once in a while someone will be getting along swimmingly with me. As soon as they find out my age, I never hear from them again. Coincidence or is it age discrimination? The only thing that stopped them from communicating with me was my age. When they didn't know what my age was, they were on me like nobody's business.

If you're a heterosexual woman or a homosexual man, the age discrimination is noticed more than any other demographic. Heterosexual men have it easier than anyone on the planet in that respect. Have no worry since there are a great deal of potentials who desire someone older, stable, and wiser when it comes to relationships.

At the same time, I've added in my age during other social experiments and managed to debunk the myth of age discrimination being present. This is due to matching with nearly a thousand potential matches of all ages from 18 to 65. They know my age as it is there in big gigantic neon numbers. Those who are ageist tend to be in the minority. They scream the loudest in the media, so it's heard in a bigger way fooling one into believing it's the norm. When you hear the darkness of ego screaming loudly about anything in any demographic, understand that you're witnessing the minority and that not everyone is that way. The ego screams with a tantrum like fury, while the truth is calm, assertive, and centered.

Dating grew to be challenging as the world moved into the technological age. Candidates have the unrealistic lists of what they want in someone, such as those who are older protest to wanting someone younger. Eventually you're not going to be fifty-five and attracting in a twenty-four-year-old for a long-term relationship unless of course you're someone like a Hugh Hefner type.

Popular culture and the media have emphasized someone as desirable when they're between the ages of 18-25. After that, you're expected to be cast out to pasture. The irony is that those aged 18-25 are generally not relationship material or ready for anything serious with anyone long term that lasts a lifetime. They don't know what they want even though in the moment they might believe they do. There is more abrupt, reckless, enacted decision making during that age period. You're also not as wise as you think you are at that moment. When I was twenty-one, I thought I was the all-knowing King. By the time I hit thirty-one and looked back on that twenty-one-year-old self, I could pity him for thinking he had it down.

The 1990's were the transition time into the technological age. It was also the point of Earth being on its last leg of the dark ages. Post 2000's showcased a change in the Earthly progressive culture stratosphere. Pre-1990 an eighteen-year-old might have known what they wanted or at least what they were supposed to do. For centuries up until that point, someone was considered as mature as a thirty-year-old by the time they were eighteen. They were going to war, getting married, buying a house, being promoted. Now someone who is eighteen is the equivalent of a child. This might be harsh criticism, but it is the reality. The opportunities are not as plentiful as they once were because there are more people on the planet and not enough jobs to fulfill that demand. It was stuck in the minds of the masses that they were intended to procreate. Procreate sure, but don't go crazy with it to the point that the planet has over 7 billion people on it. That's more akin to chaos rather than being plentiful and positively abundant. There are not enough jobs to satisfy that many people. Humankind is taking longer to mature, while some never develop all that much at all.

What someone wants under twenty-five years old will change drastically every year or two. They're also not established or have not realized their dreams, unless they're one of those rare people in the entertainment industry who hit monetary success in their twenties. Monetary success doesn't equate to spiritual success. As one moves into their later twenties and early thirties, they start to think more about the direction their life is headed down and what they want. They're a stronger candidate for a relationship at that point.

Those who identity as heterosexual men in my studies have informed me that as they aged past thirty-five years old that they reached a place where they were ready to settle down and desired a family. Except they found that most women they are interested in are not thinking of children. This causes some confusion since public opinion emphasizes that women want children. Sure they desired children in big numbers pre-2000, but since then more women have been thinking less about bringing up children, and looking more at enjoying their life or becoming professionally established. Having children is no longer at the top of their list. This doesn't mean if you have children that you're not enjoying your life. Some people find having children as being fulfilling. It is one of their life purposes here to bring up a child soul who will make positive contributions towards the betterment of humanity.

Most men, regardless of their sexual orientation, who move into their 40's and beyond tend to want someone younger who is around 27-34. Yet, those in the 27-34-age bracket are focused on trying to get their life established if it hasn't happened by then. Pre-1970, the 18-25-age bracket was the equivalent of the 27-34-age bracket of the early 2000's.

The 27-34 year olds post-2000's feel the pressure of life as they grow more aware that they're no longer twenty-two years old. A love relationship is typically not on their mind, but achieving some measure of professional success is. Love relationships are happening later in life if at all now because of that.

It used to be that people had a pretty good idea of what they wanted by age 25. This has been pushed into the late twenties and early thirties. If you don't know what you want in your 20's, then have no fear as you're right where you need to be. When it comes to careers, many switch professions on an average of three times throughout the duration of their life. Your goals and professional interests at 25 are much different than when you're 45.

The flipside of all this is that people are more youthful than they used to be, which is why we're seeing candidates in the media who are in their 40's and 50's and above looking more desirable than they would have pre-1970 at that same age. They're taking care of themselves better than past generations. They're more youthful appearing and have a child at heart like energy. Because of that, they tend to be attracted to those who are of a similar nature and around their age or younger. While those who are mature and younger are finding they're attracted to the older one who exudes playful childlike energy, but has their life together. It's a winning combo that many attempt to achieve.

If you're not bouncy and playful in your 40's and 50's and beyond, then you may have a bit of a struggle trying to get someone younger than you, unless it's a mature twenty-late something year old. The exception is if you have money since that's the allure of someone younger wanting to be taken care of. Then there are those who are of any age looking for someone who is stable and together. The prime candidates that fit that criteria are aged 35 and above.

Some say a woman is having fun up until she hits around 35, then she wants to settle down with a man who is in his 40's and above, but those men want someone younger around 27-34. The 27-34 age group are figuring out what they want and are not quite ready to settle down the way they would've been pre-1970.

This is one of the long lists of reasons that people are currently single and struggling to find a love mate connection. It's now so vastly complex that there is no tried and true reason why. You'd have to line the entire planet up and interview them about every composite of themselves. Since this would be impossible, we're resorting to the generalizations.

You should have a pretty good idea of what you want in a love relationship by the time you're 25 and at the latest by 30. Don't wait until you're 35 and beyond because that might be met with disappointment when you discover that the dating age pool is not what you expected it to be. While some don't care about age either way, it's been brought to my attention that this is a concern for many in the current dating market.

Avoid focusing on having an age preference of who you prefer to date, because people end up involved with someone that would not be what they would have initially chosen anyway. The more you limit your standards and criteria, the more likely it will be difficult in obtaining that.

As I entered my 30's and above, my age criteria on my list was someone around my age or older, but those who I ended up in a serious love relationship with were younger. They also did not have the qualities I would have necessarily listed on my requirements for a marriage mate. This is why it's best to keep an open mind and avoid the general list of statistical requirements, since as stated most people don't end up in long term romantic relationships with what they were requesting anyway. When two people hit it off on a personal level, any stats are thrown out the window and it no longer matters except the deep bond developed.

Soul connections have no egotistical human data applied to it. It's a soul connection because it's the souls connecting regardless of who they are this lifetime. This is regardless if they are six feet or five foot six, or forty-four years old, or twenty-eight, or male or female.

The darkness of ego is what is obsessed with age. Wrap your mind around the truth that every human body is aging every second. There is no way to prevent or stop that from happening and nor is anyone exempt from it, including those that harshly criticize someone who is older and losing their physical prowess as they age. People gain weight, lose their hair, lose muscle mass, develop lines and wrinkles, and so on. This is just the way human beings have been created. Accept it and look beyond all that. Those that have a challenging time accepting that are the ones that end up struggling and have a harder time than anyone else when they do reach older age. You could say in a sense that it is their Karma.

*Y*ou are a soul in a human body for a variety of purposes that include, but not limited to, learning lessons in order to grow your soul's life force, and teaching others valuable philosophies to enhance that particular soul. The physical body you inhabit does and will age and deteriorate, and then your soul exits that body.

The lower evolved navigating through life primarily from the darkness of ego call others in popular culture negative names for doing what they love. This is specifically darted at women in larger numbers, where name calling is darted their way such as old hag, grandma, or gross. The lower evolved soul views life and their surroundings in a limited way. They go along with whatever they were taught instead of breaking out of that and developing a broader view.

Popular culture plays a huge part in the development of newer generations of people. They have a huge responsibility to ensure that what they are putting out there is of sound mind and positive benefit. They've created generations of people with a limited view and this is evident in what's popular in entertainment. A mindless cliché blockbuster movie makes more money than an intelligent humanity character driven piece. Having a limited view was understandably acceptable during archaic times when humankind was not as evolved, but if this is where humankind is after all of these centuries later, then that's pretty pitiful. It's not that difficult to educate and challenge yourself by paying attention to everything that is around you. This includes seeking out ways to improve your overall mind, body, and spirit.

My Spirit team does not see age the way human ego sees age. Age has no relevance beyond knowing the stats or data of how many Earth years you've accumulated in your current life's class. There is no time limit to do anything you desire. Following your hearts calling is being connected to the Divine at any age. Never measure that with someone who might have started earlier or later. Everyone has their own path that leads to the same destination.

Spirit does not care about someone's age difference with their partner. They say age difference is irrelevant for many reasons. There is someone's human age and one's soul age, both of which are vastly different. Someone can be thirty-four years old in human years, but their soul might be one hundred and sixty-seven. It is easy to detect if someone's soul age is much older than their human age. These are people who seem wise beyond their years otherwise known as an old soul.

When I was a teenager in High School, my peers used to comment, *"You seem to know so much more than adults know, but you're a kid in High School. That's pretty cool."*

I was sixteen years old in human years, who looked like a thirteen-year-old, but felt to be nearly four hundred years old due to the instant knowledge embedded into my consciousness and perception of Earthly life.

*T*here are two people in a love relationship with one another. One of them is twenty-seven and the other is forty-two. When you observe them, the forty-two-year-old is younger in spirit, but the twenty-seven-year-old comes off like someone older than their years. They come off as if they're hundreds of years old. This would play a factor into why the twenty-seven-year-old was drawn to someone older than them, when in spiritual truth they are actually older than the forty-two-year-old in soul years.

Any two souls who feel a consenting love for one another knows God by this act. This is regardless of gender, age, race, and so on. Those who take offense over a couple's age difference govern their life by the dark part of their ego. The only thing that matters is the love between two souls. If stats are an issue for someone, then that is going along with what societal customs have dictated and trained them to follow and believe. It has no bases of truth in reality. Only the ego mind would seek to destroy the love connection made between two people regardless of the dynamic and statistical differences. Age difference concerns are a value created by humankind, but it has nothing to do with God. All souls are equal regardless of the statistical differences or how they appear.

Heaven doesn't care if someone is twenty-two and their love partner is forty-five. If it's two consenting adults who have a mutual love and appreciation for one another, then that's always applauded and supported, especially on a planet that is lacking in love. Anything or anyone who takes issue with it is operating from their lower self. Those in relationships where they have a wider gap in human age with their partner will generally not be swayed by public opinion. When there is mutual love between two people, then nothing can stop them from trying to be together no matter how forbidden it appears to the darkness of ego. It didn't stop Romeo and Juliet, nor will it stop the couple.

From a practical perspective, there are roadblocks and hurdles for a couple where one is twenty-two and the other is forty-five. They're in different places in their lives going through different circumstances, but sometimes if the younger person is an old soul and the older person is a younger soul, it brings them together and balances it out.

Two people in a relationship can be the same age and have bigger problems than an age difference. Spirit would rather see two people in a loving committed relationship and having an age difference, than not seeing humankind experiencing a loving union with anyone, especially in a world that lacks in close intimacy between two people.

The darkness of ego in humankind will have a tantrum when they disagree with the dynamics and traits of the two people in a love relationship. It isn't anyone's business, except for the two people who have formed a consented bond together. This is whether there is an age difference, it's a same sex gender union, interracial relationship, or a Christian with someone who is Jewish, and so on. The ego in humankind prefers that people be in relationships with someone who is a clone of that person. Avoid paying any attention to the ego in humankind since their views are not based in reality or spiritual truth. Spiritual truth points to the two souls who find one another and connect regardless of the labels that human beings made up and passed around.

Ive conducted endless interviews with younger people who are in relationships with older people to find out what the draw was from a practical level. The reasons why they were attracted were across the board. This applies to someone in their twenties being involved with someone over thirty-five.

Generally, someone thirty-five and older has their stuff together. This would not apply to the fifty year-old who has no relationship experience, no drive, or ambition, and no spiritual essence.

The older partner is more together, wiser, communicative, accepting, and not to mention better at love making and sex. Younger people, especially guys, tend to only be interested in getting off, rather than prolonging the lovemaking. Those desiring more passion and substance are turned off by the stiff robotic kind of sex. The attraction to someone older for this particular younger person is that they are with someone who knows what they're doing. The evolved older person is looking for more than just getting off.

Older people tend to be able to carry a conversation. This isn't totally set in stone because there are forty-six year olds who use one or two word responses, while a twenty-eight-year-old writes long paragraphs with substance. These are the exceptions, but mostly an older person can carry a conversation on many topics rather than one topic that entails wondering if you're horny or not.

The older you are, the more set in your ways you might be, but the positive of that is you can spot a phony a mile away. You're a better judge of character and don't allow just anyone into your world. When I was in my twenties, my choices were less strict, but with that came tempestuous drama filled connections.

As I grew older, my battles were picked rather than wasting time on every petty little thing in my eye line.

The more experienced older one has been around the block and knows what makes a good relationship. They were dragged through the trenches enough times to know better. They have leadership qualities rather than following the crowd in order to be popular. The older one who toots his own horn IS more popular in the end.

All of these positive traits apply to an older person who has evolved and has their life together. They're in a centered, calm, and peaceful state. While the younger person may help the older one lighten up if they're rigid and too set in their ways. They'll help them out of their comfort zone. These match ups have an entirely different teacher-student soul dynamic on other levels than if they were the same age.

CHAPTER SEVENTEEN

CRUSHING ON LOVE

Being in love is a thrilling, joyful, and exciting feeling that only those who have experienced understand the depths it can reach. This is why so many people long to be in a love relationship or have a lover, because they crave that consistent feeling of happiness that the experience brings. In essence, when you are in love with someone, it is the same feeling as having a crush. Crushes never seem to be as intense and profound as they are when you're a teenager.

You've likely felt those strong intense crushing feelings over someone who has no idea you feel that way. You wonder if you have a shot at obtaining them, or if they even feel the same way. The idea of having a crush sounds exotic initially, but they're called crushes because they can crush and hurt you emotionally. This is especially the case if the person you have a crush on doesn't return those feelings.

You're lusting after someone in an intense way

that it plagues your thoughts and feelings on a daily basis. Often the person you have a crush on has no idea you feel that way about them. In some cases, they are aware of it, but may not return the same feelings. This can be as painful as having a crush on someone who has no idea you're crushing on them. You have no idea what they think of you or if they notice you and feel the same way. In the 1984 teen High School heartthrob movie, *Sixteen Candles*, the lead melancholy isolated protagonist sixteen-year-old says about her crush, "He doesn't even know I exist."

Crushes are not always unrealistic as there are a great many circumstances where crushes have turned into more than that if you're lucky. There were a couple of my past love relationships that started out with me having a crush on them in the beginning. It seemed as if I was alone in that feeling until one day it turned out they had a crush on me too! There is no greater feeling than getting lucky and ending up in a relationship with someone you had a mutual crush with. The both of us did something about it that started out as a simple, "Hello." One of my first books was about having a crush on someone because so many have experienced that at one time or another. It was half autobiographical and half thrown in drama called, *Jagger's Revolution*. Not all crushes are intended to happen and come to fruition. It's common to have a crush on someone who is not necessarily suited for you or you for them.

I've always been fascinated with love crushes and what propels and drives someone to want another. How much of it is lust based and how much of it is love. Initially the crush is lust based and a physical cosmic uncontrollable attraction. If you're lucky enough to obtain your crush and it moves into a long-term relationship, then the real test begins. The lust feelings begin to reduce or dissolve to a degree as you discover they no longer hold up to the ideal image you initially had of them. You know you've hit a gold mine when you and this other person continue to grow and evolve together developing many different levels of love for one another beyond the crush status.

Having confidence and believing that your crush would date you is optimistic and puts that positive energy out there. It's wise to have some measure of reality in check so as not to get hurt, or to push it to the point where you're stalking your crush. You're attracted to someone and your heart starts racing. You get nervous, sweaty, all thumbs, quiet, your head is down, you check your phone, and are evasive. You're doing everything except looking at the person you have a crush on and confidently saying, "Hello. What's up?"

If you're not looking at the person you have a crush on, or you pretend to not see them, then nothing will happen. They'll assume why bother as you don't appear to be interested. They will feel as if they're barking up the wrong tree. Put in an effort by looking at them and say, "Hello."

If they look the other way or don't answer you, then you have to gauge whether they are interested, but are guarded and shy, or they're not interested and trying to make that known by coming off disinterested. You can see how mixed signals can be put out that confuse someone. When you have a crush on someone, then you want to believe they feel it too, so the ego immediately goes into, "Well, they're probably crushing on me too, but are terribly shy."

When you come to the realization that perhaps

they don't have any interest or attraction to you, then you can say, "At least I tried and now I have my answer."

You can quickly move on to the next victim until you have a match. All of the serious love relationships I've had over the course of my life happened when I wasn't looking or intending to connect with anyone new. This is for those who obsess over wondering when *the one* will show up. The desperation is what blocks it from happening. Love relationships happen when you least expect it.

You take your time getting to know someone and then you strike gold, otherwise you experience disappointment, shock, and heartache. You rush in with a new person abruptly without truly taking the time to get to know the object you have your eye on "in person" gradually. Most of the time, the connection ends just as unexpectedly as it began.

You cannot rush love even after you've met someone new. Two people need time to get to know one another before jumping into something as a committed relationship or marriage. You cannot force someone to like you and go out with you, but what you can do is put in an effort and see what happens.

The way that love and relationships happen will continue to change as time moves on and generations evolve. This is currently a time where it's equally easy as well as challenging to find a connection that goes the distance. You've basically got a 50/50 shot. When you are lucky enough to fall for someone who is falling for you too, then you will both want to honor that, treasure it, care about it, and continue to invest in it. There is no magic wand to make love happen for someone if the world is ruled primarily by ego. Not even Heaven can fight that due to the universal spirit law of free will that human souls are governed by.

You have a strong growing love for someone and you don't know why. Perhaps the logistics are not in your favor. You or this other person is in a relationship, you have a large age difference, or you live far away from one another whether it be another county, state, or country altogether. Explore it to see if this other person truly is the one you're intended to be with.

You are responsible for you. When you give up that independence because you enter into a love relationship and become reliant on that person, then that is no longer love, but dependency. Due to the free will law, you place yourself in situations as a result of your choices and actions. This is one of the lessons you're faced with when it comes back to bite you. You discover the reality is you put yourself in a situation that didn't turn out the way you hoped. No one can be blamed for the decisions that someone makes as an adult. You can't blame the person you chose to get into a relationship with. You cannot blame a higher power, your Spirit team, or God for not helping you out of your situation. You can ask for Heavenly assistance, but they're not going to help in ways that do not benefit your higher self. They will relay action steps, such as coming out of sloth mode, looking for a job, or getting healthy again in order to get you and your energy moving. If you're not following the guidance that reveals the path to take, then there is only so much they can be done.

The fear energy surrounding not being in a love relationship is so great that it feels like a huge impossible hurdle to overcome. People stay in unhappy relationships for security reasons or familiarity. They're afraid to get out of it as that would require change. Avoid the fear that accompanies making a change, but welcome it and take action steps that can lead you to the freedom that change offers.

It may be a loveless world, but there are still a great many souls coming together in relationships everyday within the confinement of it. You cannot ditch love entirely, because love is present beneath the layers of all souls regardless if they choose to find ways to access it or not. Love never dies in this sense. You can say you want to focus on work or on yourself, but the bottom line is when a relationship is intended to happen, it will come about unexpectedly regardless if it messes up with your goals to achieve. You can still succeed while in a relationship. Being in the right connection motivates you to accomplish more and reach higher heights, so it's a win-win.

Another key trait applied towards a successful relationship is following through. You don't do things for your partner because you have to. You do them because you want to. You both need chemistry, compatibility, communication, and commitment to make it work. It's always bliss in the beginning of a love relationship because you don't really know the person you're dating. You are enamored and curious about this new person you know nothing about. Everyone puts their best face forward in the beginning, but soon you get sloppy and the real you is revealed. Whoever loves that real you is the keeper. Eventually you get to know the other person pretty well to a good degree. This is when the real test begins on whether it truly is love. How you merge together as a team and a couple and forge forward as one is the true testament to it being real love or not.

Sometimes connections are intended to end when they have run their course. Other times, one or both people operate on free will, which ultimately plays a hand at dissolving the union. Getting close to a perfect union is where you're both experiencing the same love with one another. You're both facing the same direction and you support and love each other. There's little to no drama and arguments, since you accept each other's flaws. There will be turbulence and challenges in a perfect union at times, which is to be expected. When those who are in a perfect union come to the epicenter of discord, then they naturally find a way to smooth out the edges and return back to that perfect state of being. This is something to thrive for in any partnership since how you manage through crises together shows the strength and possibilities of a relationship.

If you're single and frustrated, then do your best to make the most of it. Partake in activities that continue to make you smile, live life, showcase your best self, put in an effort if you see someone you want to know. Get out there and stay optimistic and have faith that love will happen and that love is all around you no matter where you go. All of those clichés were said throughout entertainment history in love songs and romantic films, because they were true. Someone experienced those feelings firsthand. They wrote a hit song about it or a screenplay for a romantic movie because love inspires the masses when they allow it to penetrate into their soul. The planet is starved for affection. It's obvious by the way others treat one another. The negative words being darted around all over the media. The remote distance the masses exude and the lack of true tolerance and acceptance.

Affectionate human contact is desired deep down in the heart of all souls.

Cuddling, hugging, and touching have immense therapeutic properties. These acts assist to bring down your cortisol levels more rapidly than anything else. When you engage in these activities with someone, or your romantic partner, it assists in lightening the load or dissolving traces of unhappiness, stress, or upset. It raises your vibration and boosts oxytocin levels, which is the love drug hormone that calms your entire body and expands the soul's light. Even if you don't have a love partner, then hugging a friend or a pet can offer the same benefits.

Being physically touched and kissed repeatedly is like oxygen to me. It has the same endorphin release one gets through exercise. I am a walking love bug Casanova after all, which in the past has been a handful or detrimental when I placed it in the hands of the passion-less, the unromantic, or the non-committal.

Partaking in love activities such as regular touch can open up your *clair* channels to receive clearer guidance and messages from above in this state. Being in love releases the dopamine and oxytocin hormones. What's erupted are upbeat feelings that create an overall sense of positive well-being. You're basically high on life! You're more focused and energetic able to accomplish things that you had previously put aside before you experienced Earth's saving miracle called love. Love is like a drug, but a healthy one that gives you a natural high that no vice, cigarette, drink, drug, or bad food can offer or reach.

Like the song, remember to let your love flow like a mountain stream...

SOUL MATES AND TWIN FLAMES
Available in paperback and E-book
by Kevin Hunter

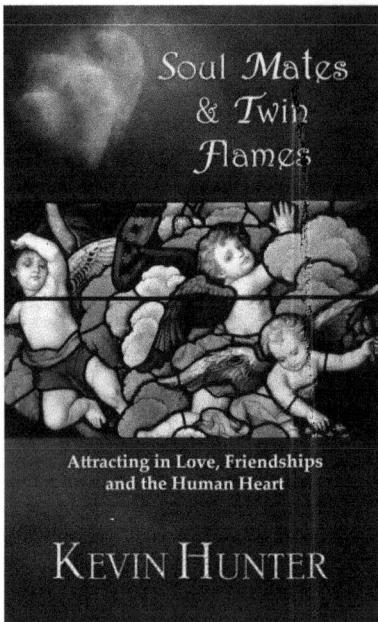

Everyone is interested in love and relationships whether they like to admit it or not. Even the most hardened human soul has fantasized about having a love interest or a partner in crime. One of the main reasons you are here is to love and to learn how to love. This is not just in intimate relationships, but with everyone you come into contact with.

In, *Soul Mates and Twin Flames*, author **Kevin Hunter** touches on the topic of love and relationships by passing on some of the messages and guidance he has received from his own Guides and Angels on the topic.

Included in this informational book are some of the basics on Soul Mates, Twin Flames, Dysfunctional Relationships, Reconnecting with an Ex, Karmic Relationships, Friendships, Loneliness, working with the Romance Angels, Dating, Relationships, and more.

Also available in paperback and E-book
by Kevin Hunter,
"Warrior of Light: Messages from my Guides and Angels"

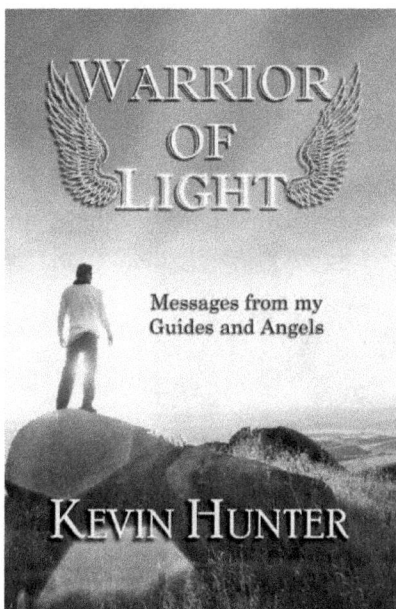

There are legions of angels, spirit guides, and departed loved ones in heaven that watch and guide you on your journey here on Earth. They are around to make your life easier and less stressful. Do you pay attention to the nudges, guidance, and messages given to you? There are many who live lives full of negativity and stress while trying to make ends meet. This can shake your faith as it leads you down paths of addictions, unhealthy life choices, and negative relationship connections. Learn how you can recognize the guidance of your own Spirit team of guides and angels around you.

Author, Kevin Hunter, relays heavenly guided messages about getting humanity, the world, and yourself into shape. He delivers the guidance passed onto him by his own Spirit team on how to fine tune your body, soul and raise your vibration. Doing this can help you gain hope and faith in your own life in order to start attracting in more abundance.

Available in paperback and E-book
by Kevin Hunter,
*"Empowering Spirit Wisdom: A Warrior of Light's Guide on
Love, Career and the Spirit World"*

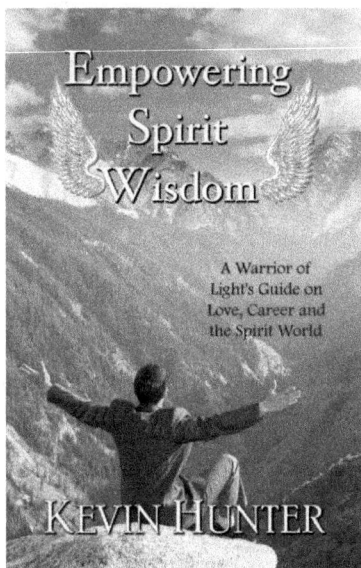

Kevin Hunter relays heavenly, guided messages for everyday life concerns with his book, *Empowering Spirit Wisdom*. Some of the topics covered are your soul, spirit and the power of the light, laws of attraction, finding meaningful work, transforming your professional and personal life, navigating through the various stages of dating and love relationships, as well as other practical affirmations and messages from the Archangels. Kevin Hunter passes on the sensible wisdom given to him by his own Spirit team in this inspirational and powerful book.

Available in paperback and E-book
by Kevin Hunter,
"Realm of the Wise One"

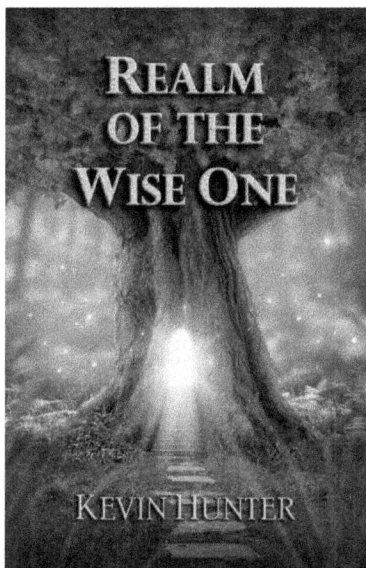

In the Spirit Worlds and the dimensions that exist, reside numerous kingdoms that house a plethora of Spirits that inhabit various forms. One of these tribes is called the Wise Ones, a darker breed in the spirit realm who often chooses to incarnate into a human body one lifetime after another for important purposes.

The *Realm of the Wise One* takes you on a magical journey to the spirit world where the Wise Ones dwell. This is followed with in-depth and detailed information on how to recognize a human soul who has incarnated from the Wise One Realm. Author, Kevin Hunter, is a Wise One who uses the knowledge passed onto him by his Spirit team of Guides and Angels to relay the wisdom surrounding all things Wise One. He discusses the traits, purposes, gifts, roles, and personalities among other things that make up someone who is a Wise One. Wise Ones have come in the guises of teachers, shaman, leaders, hunters, mediums, entertainers and others. *Realm of the Wise One* is an informational guide devoted to the tribe of the Wise Ones, both in human form and on the other side.

Available in paperback and E-book
by Kevin Hunter,
"Darkness of Ego"

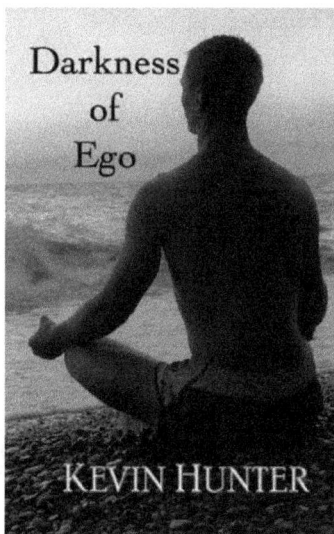

The biggest cause of turmoil and conflict in one's life is executed by the human ego. All souls have an ego. The unruliest and destructive ego exists within every human soul. When the soul enters into a physical human body, the ego immediately compresses and then swells up. It is the higher self's goal to ensure that it remains in check while living an Earthly life. The ego is what tests each soul along its journey. It is how one learns right from wrong.

In *Darkness of Ego*, author Kevin Hunter infuses some of the guidance, messages, and wisdom he's received from his Spirit team surrounding all things ego related. The ego is one of the most damaging culprits in human life. Therefore, it is essential to understand the nature of the beast in order to navigate gracefully out of it when it spins out of control. Some of the topics covered in *Darkness of Ego* are humanity's destruction, mass hysteria, karmic debt, and the power of the mind, heaven's gate, the ego's war on love and relationships, and much more.

The *Warrior of Light* series of pocket books
are available in paperback and E-book
by Kevin Hunter

Spirit Guides and Angels, Soul Mates and Twin Flames,
Raising Your Vibration, Divine Messages for Humanity,
Connecting with the Archangels, The Seven Deadly Sins

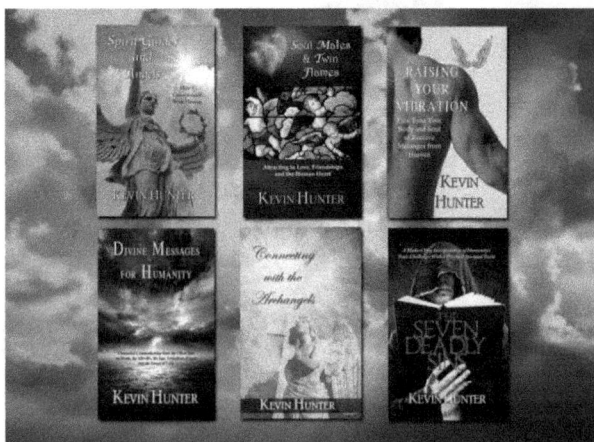

Also available in paperback and E-book by Kevin Hunter, *Ignite Your Inner Life Force* and *Awaken Your Creative Spirit*

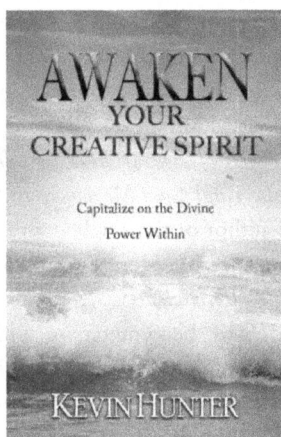

About the Author

Kevin Hunter is an author, love expert, and channeler. His books tackle a variety of genres and tend to have a strong male protagonist. The messages and themes he weaves in his work surround Spirit's own communications of love and respect which he channels and infuses into his writing and stories.

His spiritually based empowerment books include, *Warrior of Light, Empowering Spirit Wisdom, Realm of the Wise One, Reaching for the Warrior Within, Darkness of Ego, Ignite Your Inner Life Force, Awaken Your Creative Spirit, Tarot Card Meanings,* and *The Seven Deadly Sins.* He is also the author of the single dating guide *Love Party of One*, the horror, drama, *Paint the Silence*, and the modern day erotic love story, *Jagger's Revolution.*

Before becoming an author, Kevin started out in the entertainment business in 1996 becoming actress Michelle Pfeiffer's personal development dude for her boutique production company, Via Rosa Productions. She dissolved her company after several years and he made a move into coordinating film productions for the big studios on such films as *One Fine Day, A Thousand Acres, The Deep End of the Ocean, Crazy in Alabama, The Perfect Storm, Original Sin, Harry Potter & the Sorcerer's Stone, Dr. Dolittle 2* and *Carolina.* He considers himself a beach bum born and raised in Southern California.

For more information, www.kevin-hunter.com